HOW TO WIN

Also by the Secret Footballer:

I Am the Secret Footballer
Tales from the Secret Footballer
The Secret Footballer's Guide to the Modern Game
Access All Areas

THE SECRET FOOTBALLER

WITH THE SECRET PSYCHOLOGIST

HOW TO WIN

LESSONS FROM THE PREMIER LEAGUE

First published in 2017
by Guardian Books, Kings Place, 90 York Way, London N1 9GU
and Faber & Faber Ltd, Bloomsbury House,
74–77 Great Russell Street, London WC1B 3DA

This paperback edition published in the UK in 2017
This paperback edition published in the US in 2017

2 4 6 8 10 9 7 5 3 1

A CIP record for this book is available from the British Library

ISBN 978–1–78335–124–4

Typeset by seagulls.net
Printed and bound by CPI Group (UK) Ltd, Croydon, CR0 4YY

*Publisher's note: Some identifying features have been altered
in this book to protect the Secret Footballer's identity.*

'We are because we win. If we lose we no longer exist.'

EDUARDO GALEANO, *Soccer in Sun and Shadow*

For Shakeel

A creative, a visionary and an inspiration –
a powerhouse of positive thinking

1956–2015

CONTENTS

FOREWORD

By Mrs TSF

When my husband announced that he was writing a book with a psychologist I assumed that the subject would be me. How have I coped? Do I use confirmation bias to justify a hasty selection in the mating department? To what extent do I use hindsight to minimise the effects of catastrophe? Is my general state of mind closer to acceptance than it is to anger?

My husband is a very complex man. But you've probably got that already.

I get to write the Foreword. God knows what comes after that.

He can be such a little boy at times, but then he displays a schizophrenic agility that lets him pivot 180 degrees and go toe-to-toe with anybody on any subject in any arena. Even if he knows nothing about it.

I knew him before he became a footballer. I knew him when he had nothing. He has always been the same. At his old place of work he taunted the bosses with his humour and they hated him for it. Personally, and this is hard for me to say, I know that he enjoys mentally messing with people who think that he is beneath them. Some people can't take it. They will cry like little babies. Others will run out of words and stick their fists up and fight. A few will run off and cry to somebody in authority.

My husband's weapon of choice is to mentally wear the person down to a tiny nub.

When my husband became a footballer there were inevitable fallings-out with people in positions of power. He always questions authority before he respects it. Most of the authority figures in football didn't have the right answers.

Once, he was told that he had to train with the youth team for the rest of the season after throwing a huff when he'd been substituted in a big Premier League game. He reckoned he must have been the highest-paid youth-team player in history. For some people that thought would be enough. Money coming in. Who cares?

He embarked on revenge through psychological warfare, however. Every morning he walked out with the first team on to their training pitch and began warming up with them. The manager would send over one of his coaches to tell my husband that he had to go over and train with the youth team. Using a minion to do his dirty work. My husband never budged.

'Tell him to come over here and tell me to train with the youth-team squad himself if that's what he wants.'

The poor minion would run back and relay the message. The manager would trudge over in front of everybody to tell my husband what he had told him yesterday and the day before.

'Go and train with the youth team.'

And my husband would smile and turn away.

'No problem.'

He would jog off at a gentle pace towards the youth-team pitch, leaving behind a manager grinding his teeth and a first-team squad smiling to themselves. It was like Paul Newman tormenting the warden in *Cool Hand Luke*.

I know that the manager never really recovered. He did the small man's trick of trying to bully other people around the club to make himself feel tall. He wound up telling the team chef how to cook. One day he physically assaulted a player. The media got to hear about it. My husband can be very open about things when he feels like it. Shortly afterwards, the club announced that it had come to a mutually beneficial decision to terminate the manager's contract.

Winning that war made my husband happy for a while but, generally, he is not a happy man. He is a calculating and decisive person and a lot of the time he is plain depressed. Like most footballers, he has an ego but he also has a huge fear of lots of the people around him. He hates talking to people because he thinks he's being recorded. He doesn't trust anybody and he is fiercely protective of himself.

As I say, he is a complex man.

That's what makes him who he is. All the backdoors and nooks and crannies in his personality. He is always interesting to me. He never pandered to a crowd just hoping that more people might like him. His clubs, managers and the fans always had to take him on his own terms, even if that wasn't the most profitable way for him to operate. There were times when I wanted him just to be like everybody else. It would have been easier for him. Mostly, though, I loved the difference.

By the time he became a footballer, it was too late for football to realise that he wasn't the same as everybody else. He didn't go through an academy or a youth system in his teens. He'd lived in the real world. When football let him through the door it didn't know quite what it was getting.

He felt, and still feels, that all of the footballers who went before him simply didn't get it. He has told me often that in England the virtues that make a winning player are completely against the grain of what English people admire in their heroes. The British public don't outwardly support anything or anyone until winning is a foregone conclusion, and at that moment certain rough edges – if that's what you want to call them – are overlooked and forgiven. The person doing the winning needs to stay alert, though. The crowd can turn on them in a flash.

He always tells me that Lewis Hamilton is a winner but that he isn't liked by much of the British population because of his intense will to win and his selfishness in the way that he achieves success. His mentality is the same as Michael Schumacher's was, but because Schumacher is foreign his attitude is acceptable.

He can reel them off: Stephen Hendry is another, a genius who wasn't loved by the British public despite dominating his sport, snooker. People preferred Jimmy White.

My husband reckons this country demands tragic characters who lose (but only by a narrow margin) and not relentless winners. There's a hill at Wimbledon named after Tim Henman. Wasn't it Andy Murray who actually won the thing, though? Bit up himself, isn't he? Wouldn't hurt him to smile, would it? And what's with the mother? Sure, he's British when he wins Wimbledon, but should he lose the final of the Cincinnati Masters then he's definitely Scottish.

When my husband hit the big time, or the big time hit him (I've never been sure which), he was a 23-year-old kid. And people suddenly decided that he was something of a hero. Fans of the club he was with were desperate for somebody to come along and change things, but they had been drip-fed a line of players who were incapable of pushing the club to the next level. Yes, 'they ran through walls' and 'they tackled anything that moved'. They were good old-fashioned British footballing stock and made the right noises, but never had the talent necessary to change anything.

When things started gaining traction at the club, word of mouth spread around the city to the fans, via the local media, and through to the TV networks like Sky. Something different was happening in this unfashionable corner of planet football. And my husband was in the vanguard, pulling people along while others waited to be pushed. He was different by nature and by design. He enjoyed being considered odd. He was cold, hard-nosed and dislikeable right the way through it all. He patronised the media who asked stupid questions and he was indifferent towards those people who queued up to talk about football with him. He got the job done on the pitch. He didn't act like a cliché off it.

In football they have little motivational sayings that they like to plaster on the walls of changing rooms:

BE RUTHLESS
BE BRUTAL

The problem is that there aren't many people, even in football, who truly understand just how ruthless and brutal you have to be; there are even fewer who are prepared to be that way.

I married one of the ones who understood. That's just part of his personality, though.

I might ask him more about it when he finishes doing his household chores and brings me my cup of tea. Meanwhile, read on. Put your wellies on and yomp through the messed-up psychology of football and footballers.

INTRODUCTION

By TSF

OK, OK, I get it. You're sat there with this book in your hands thinking to yourself, 'Seriously? What the fuck does TSF know about psychology? Why did I spend my Amazon book voucher on this?'

I understand. What footballers know about the outside world is what they see on the front page of the *Sun* while their mate is reading the back page. Isn't it?

Well, my qualifications for a football psychology book are informal. I know football. I inhabited the changing rooms and the training pitches and the stadiums for a long, long time. I saw men under pressure. I saw men succeed and more men fail. I always wondered where the difference lay. Why did Kevin Keegan crack? When did it go bad for Fernando Torres? How could Kenny Dalglish let himself be made to look a fool by Luis Suárez? Why did some players love the big match days while others trembled? Why was it that some guys couldn't get it done on afternoons when they were expected to thrive, but always came through when they were rank underdogs? Why are some players utter world-beaters in training and a universal letdown in a professional match?

I always wondered about these things. So I read books and talked to people and kept mental notes in a filing cabinet in my head. So no, I have not been to Harvard. I haven't published academic theories for peer review. But I have lived some and learned lots. I don't expect this book will make the syllabus at Harvard, but it will be referred to often in student theses.

Outside of football, psychology is one of the subjects that really stimulates me. In fact, many of the guys I played alongside who had hopes of becoming coaches or managers shared my fascination. We always knew that football was about so much more than just getting the best players and putting them out on the pitch. Some managers ruled through terror. Some managers cajoled through compliments and encouragement. The smartest ones knew who would respond to terror and who would respond to praise, and dished both out accordingly.

I wasn't one of those kids who got signed up to a football club at the age of nine and never thought about anything else from then till retirement. For a long time, it looked as if my life was going in a different direction entirely to football, and that's when I became interested in reading about psychology. An unexamined life isn't worth living, and I was interested in understanding what made me tick, and what made the people around me tick, and how I could navigate a way through life to find some sort of success or happiness.

I've tried to apply little bits of what I have learned to most of what I've done. I'm a layman, though. My understanding of psychology only goes so far. In fact, just far enough to understand that my understanding only goes so far. I'm not an expert but I have learned enough, generally, to get what I want from people, from situations and for myself. If that sounds selfish, well, think about it. It's what we all want. It's just that most people don't have a map to help them get there. Most people react on emotion and hope for the best. The people who you think always land on their feet are not 'lucky', they have simply taken the time to work out where they want to end up and how to manipulate the series of events that must unfold first. Most people do not give that series of events the respect it deserves. And I get that. Because it can hurt your head. It's easier simply to look ahead to the end result.

That was what drew me to psychology in the first place. Wanting to see the wood *and* the trees.

Here's a thing that catches most professional athletes unawares when they retire: the world doesn't stop turning. It hardly pauses to blink. They play the competitions anyway. The fans cheer anyway. Somebody wears the jersey you once wore and they are now part of something that you thought you were integral to. One or two of the kids who used to clean my boots became heroes at the Euros this summer. Football goes on within you and without you.

You have nothing to do all day. And the world you lived in keeps spinning and throwing up stories and excitement. So it turns out that it wasn't all about you after all. As the baseball player Jim Bouton said at the end of his brilliant book, *Ball Four*, he had spent a lifetime gripping a baseball only to realise that it was the other way around.

When I retired, they didn't stop the clocks or paint the swans black. The phone didn't ring off the hook when word slithered across the breaking-news bar on Sky Sports News. There weren't four million people signing a petition hoping to have the decision reversed.

So I said thank you and fuck you to football. I went away and more or less lost my interest in the game. I watched matches, but in a detached way. I wrote some books, read some more books, got involved in a few business deals and tried not to look back in anger or self-satisfaction too often. But between finishing the last book and beginning this one, a series of phone calls came. I took myself off the suicide list and began wondering again if the Soviet-style statue of me that the world was secretly planning should be chipped from granite or from marble.

The first call was from an ex-teammate. He phones me about once every five years and we think of that as keeping in touch. Actually, he FaceTimed me, and nobody does that unless they want to emphasise a point with jabbing fingers and rehearsed expressions of enthusiasm.

We enjoyed great success together, the two of us, hence the regularity of his phone calls.

What's that? Do I call him? Mind your own business.

For those of you who are unfamiliar with the Dunning-Kruger effect, take your notebooks out now, please. The Dunning-Kruger effect sets out to explain the cognitive bias that affects somebody who is so stupid that they lack the part of the brain that would flag to them that they are stupid in the first place.

It's the illusion of superiority.

My former teammate would not be a man to take an interest in such things, yet he reckoned that something like the Dunning-Kruger effect explained the complete lack of calls from those who knew me from my playing days. I don't mean social calls; I mean the ones with offers of fresh employment in a new role. As we FaceTimed, he was steadfast in his view that the clubs I wanted to work at weren't welcoming me with open arms because they knew me. They knew me very well.

Not that I have character flaws, dodgy attributes or some contagious tropical disease. No. Quite the reverse, in fact. (I refer you to Mrs TSF's charming Foreword.) It was, my friend told me, because they're all terrified that if I got my foot in the door, I would immediately begin sussing out how to take their jobs.

That thought lodged in my head like the fatty deposits that have lodged in my arteries since I stopped eating like an athlete.

Maybe I was on the flipside of the Dunning-Kruger effect. One of those highly skilled individuals who underestimate their own superiority and competence and assume that what comes easily to them comes just as easily to everybody else. Nobody had ever accused me of underestimating my own superiority before, but I began to think that my friend was spot-on. I looked forward to five years passing so that we could discuss it further.

Meanwhile, I would remain unemployed.

But then about a week later, completely out of the blue, the floodgates opened and I had a number of enquiries as to my availability to manage a professional football team.

I know, right? Me! Had I dumbed down or had football finally cottoned on to what it was missing?

When I say a number of enquiries, I mean two. And when I say floodgates, I mean a hairline crack in the wall. Still. There are only 92 league clubs in England and tens of millions of people across the world who want to manage them. And these two clubs were testing the waters of ME! (Forget for a moment that some of the men who are currently in charge of league clubs can't tie their shoelaces in a hurry. Pretend, as I did, that they are an elite corps.)

Me, out of everybody. Out of all the millions.

I always used to think that way when I was a player, too. It was a major confidence boost to think that out of all the professional footballers in the world, I had been chosen to play on that Saturday against Manchester United at Old Trafford in a specific position before anybody else. Me, who hadn't been anywhere near professional football when I hit my twenties.

Many would have fallen to their knees and thanked their god. I see myself more as a self-made man who worships his creator.

In fact, I think it is a mistake to go into football management too soon after the free boots stop coming from Nike. There is a learning curve that is just too steep. And lots of players-turned-managers don't even see that curve. I'm still a young man and in terms of management I'm still a teenager. Managers who go straight from playing into the hot seat are headed for trouble. Having a degree in politics doesn't make you prime minister. (Going to Eton and having the right chums maybe. OK, it was a bad analogy.)

The point is that learning curves can either be negotiated on the job, with the media laughing every time you slip, or it can be done under the wing of smart men and away from the limelight. You can, as many aspiring young coaches and managers do, take the Eton route and swing a favour, perhaps to go and spend a week with Pep Guardiola watching Manchester City train. Quite how that relates to your coaching job at Luton Town is lost on me.

For two years now I have been watching football as an ex-player. I watch football at all levels, from Barcelona to Nuneaton. I don't always learn something but I often meet people along the way, and these people invariably have the same thing to tell me: 'I had to learn on the job, it was tough, but we did as well as we could. I think I know what I'm doing now. I've learned so much. If I could just get back in and land another job somewhere, I know exactly what I have to do now.'

Too late, mate. You're tainted. Football doesn't do forgiveness. Rehab is for players only. Second chances are possible, but only for about 10 per cent. The other 90 per cent just failed to cut it. Harsh as it sounds, that is football's view.

Most players miss football so much they forget one thing: the key to remaining relevant is not to stay in the limelight but to keep in contact with the people near the limelight, those who hold positions within clubs that involve recruitment. Someday, they'll need to say to themselves, 'Hmm, what about TSF? He's smart. He could be a good fit for this club.'

That is an important lesson. Turn up at the odd training ground. Talk. Listen. Drink coffee. Ask questions. Offer advice when appropriate. Watch. See what works and what doesn't. Remember Dunning-Kruger and be smart enough to know that you are not that smart. Yet.

So take your time. The last manager to call me asked if I was ready to get back into the game yet. I replied that I am getting there but I am in no rush to take the under-21 job at Rochdale. He knew exactly what I meant. I've said so often in the past that I have no interest in going into management that I might as well have had the words tattooed on to my forehead. And yet two owners still called and chose to ignore the fact that I have no experience. The confidence boost that I took from those calls was incredible.

I started to ask myself, what would it take to be a good manager? When you are a player, every football story is a laugh or an outrage. But this has to change when you consider it from a manager's perspective. You have to ask questions. Why did that happen? How could it have been handled better? What is the fallout going to be?

Getting players to listen up and do as they're told is an art form when it is done well. Correction: it is an exercise in psychology. You have to know that every player is different. What makes each player tick and what are the dynamics within the group they are part of? How do you make them buy into what you are trying to do? When they come in on Monday morning after being thumped 4–0 on Saturday, how do you make them believe they can win?

You need the brashness to believe that your way is the right way for the entire organisation, and you need the humility to remember that a lot of what happens in football doesn't tally with what you would have done. Even if your method worked.

The job of management is more and more about psychology. How to handle young men who are rich, gifted and privileged, and who have agents and fans reminding them of that all the time.

When I look back on the best managers of my career, I realise that they were successful because they knew how to deal with every single aspect of a player's mental physique. The worst managers had absolutely no idea how to deal with people. One-size-fits-all was their view. One size of jackboot usually. They failed because they just couldn't understand people.

Some players will have a bad game every now and again. Maybe a coach will watch the video back with them and try to help with their positioning. Maybe they'll need a bollocking. Probably not. Great darts players or snooker players sometimes don't sight the shot properly and they miss what they'd ordinarily get with their eyes closed. They don't need a bollocking. They run on confidence. There are players who take each match on its merits and try to think about the best way forward, adapting parts of their game to suit the opposition. They are self-managing. Others need to be spoon-fed.

Every player is different, and harmonising all of those personalities and implementing a team-wide strategy to win a match is hugely complex. And when it goes wrong, although the manager carries the can, it's not always his fault. People have their own private emotions. They are constantly being blown off course by the environment around them. At certain moments in a football match, they are beyond the reach of any guidance or man management and for a period of time they just slip into a void.

Many modern managers don't sign their own players, though they are consulted. They have assistants who are experts in the tactical aspects of the game, so many don't take training sessions. So what is left to the manager? I'll tell you. A ruthless ability to lead a team of players into battle by manipulating their mentality and galvanizing them to win for themselves, their teammates, their club and their manager. An ability to make their team that little better than the opposition.

And that sounds easy, right? Let me tell you something, it absolutely isn't.

That is what is so fascinating.

INTRODUCTION

By the Secret Psychologist

I get asked two questions frequently. The first is: 'Can I have your autograph?' (I bear an uncanny likeness to Brad Pitt), and the second is: 'Do footballers take this psychology thing seriously?'

The second question is not conveniently answered by the fact that TSF has asked me, the Secret Psychologist, to write this book with him. It is more that increasing numbers of people are realising that the difference between those who win and those who lose is often what goes on behind the eyes. These days, psychologists working with sportsmen and women is common enough practice, so the question is not whether footballers take it seriously, it's why some other sports seem not to.

TSF talks about the kids at his school who could run fast, kick a ball better than others, were smart, or showed musical prowess. Most of those kids did not fulfil their potential. Think back to your school. I bet there was a footballer there who had the talent of TSF. A kid who was destined for big things. You would have put money on them being the one to make it. Head and shoulders above the rest – have them in the team and you won.

TSF also talks about what I call self-investment. While other kids went out partying on a Friday night, he was busy practising. While other kids were lying in on a rainy Saturday morning, he was taking penalties, perfecting accuracy by aiming at a cricket stump. This is not just a story of practising, though; this is a lesson in attitude. To practise is to have the *will* to do so. Talent is not enough. It is not talent alone that will get you to the success levels enjoyed by TSF. It is the *application* of your talent. A mindset based upon the notion of wanting to win. Wanting to be the best.

Colin Montgomerie once surprised me by saying that golf wasn't his passion. Winning was. It just so happened that in golf he had found something that he could beat other people at. He believed (in a field of 120 golfers) that to finish second was to be the first loser. If he played you at tiddly-winks he would still enjoy winning.

It's all about what you want to do with what you've got.

I got into psychology through an amateur interest. I was shit at everything, and I started to wonder why. Actually, to be more accurate, I was good at a few things, but failed spectacularly at them. The curse was not that I couldn't do them, it was that I could, but didn't!

At this point, I should tell you that I was an average sportsman, but not great – even though I was technically gifted at my sport. More interestingly, I have also been sacked from every job I have ever had. I could fulfil the roles, but it was more a matter of not fitting in. I didn't apply myself in the same way others did. Therefore, I was a disrupter, a maverick and unmanageable. (Unfortunately, disrupters get sacked. In my opinion, they should be hired.)

I started to read some books in order to better understand myself and my behaviour. I soon realised it wasn't that I was crap; it was just that corporate life wasn't for me. Instead of feeling bad about myself – which was conspiring to take me down a very dark path – I eventually understood that it wasn't me, it was them.

Psychology helped me to express my own talent. It actually worked for me. I started my own business and did things my way. I am not an academic. I am a 'try it and see what happens' sort of person. I am practical. I'm not one for theories and rah-rah-rah motivation. Positive thinking is nice ... intelligence is nicer.

And so I've applied my thoughts and advice in this book in a no-nonsense way. It is as relevant for home life and business life as it is for Premier League footballers – I figure improvement is improvement, right? I'd like you to read the psychology bits in this book and think, 'Why not?' Even if you are a sceptic. You don't have to try to bring about a sea change or do anything dramatic. There is no quick fix, gimmick or hint that will take you from the local league to the Premier League. It's about making 'one degree of change'. Having worked with some of the best businesses and sports teams in the world, I have seen great results come from marginal improvements. The one degree of change is based upon the idea that if you had two parallel lines and moved one line by one degree, the further you went along the lines the more they would diverge, and eventually there would be a huge difference in where each line finishes up.

So not everything in this book will be relevant to you, but try to pick out one or two things that resonate. These don't have to be directly targeting a problem area – just choose a thought, sentence or idea that you can make your own and have some fun with in your quest to be better.

1. ROOTS

Lessons learned early

When I was growing up there were two events which, I realise now, had a profound effect on my life. As with a lot of the things that influence us deeply, it isn't the magnitude of the event so much as the timing that causes it to leave a mark.

Both of these things happened at key moments in my adolescence, a time when change was going to happen anyway but fate just decided to stir things up a bit. Looking back now, these two events bookended my adolescence, but when you are young, shit just happens to you in apparently random order. It's only years later, when you are spring-cleaning your brain, that you pick things up, examine them in the light and put them into some perspective.

In 1988 my father decided, for reasons best known to himself, that he would take a driving trip through Holland. And that he would take me with him. Why flat, featureless Holland? And why me? Was he making flat and featureless a theme of his trip? I explained to him that if he stood on a phone book and put me on his shoulders, we would both be able to see all of Holland anyway, but he was determined that we would see every canal, dyke and wooden clog that Holland had to offer.

(I know, I know, it's really the Netherlands. Holland is only part of the country, two provinces that were once a single province called Holland. But we Brits have let Europe go it alone, so we don't worry about these petty things anymore. Anyway, in football Holland will always be Holland.)

It was the eighties and I was young, which meant that I was held captive to my father's musical tastes. When he slipped Peter Gabriel into the cassette player I feared the worst.

I was wrong. There was a piece of music in there called 'Milgram's 37' which crept up on me, threw a hood over my head and never let me go again. It had haunted cries and harsh chimes upon every chord. It was both beautiful and brutal, and it has been lodged in my head like a sliver of shrapnel ever since. 'Milgram's 37' has driven me to despair and depression and to comfort and understanding.

The song is about a set of experiments carried out by a psychologist called Stanley Milgram, a man who became a hero to me. One thing about Rihanna, Katy Perry and the like is that they don't write many songs about behavioural psychologists. More's the pity. The eighties were the golden age of psychology songs. 'Shout' by Tears for Fears was about primal therapy. John Lennon's 'Mother' had similar origins. 'Cloudbusting' by Kate Bush was about the psychologist Wilhelm Reich. 'Synchronicity II' by the Police was about

Carl Jung and U2's 'The Electric Co.' was about electro-convulsive therapy.

Anyway.

Milgram was born in 1933 in New York City and he went on to become a psychologist at Yale University. He grew up reading about the war in Europe, and every evening his family, who had relatives there, gathered around the radio to listen to the latest bulletins.

When the war ended, some family members came from Europe to stay in the Bronx; they had been in concentration camps and had numbers tattooed on their arms. This had a profound effect on Milgram. He later wrote to a friend that 'I should have been born into the German-speaking Jewish community of Prague in 1922 and died in a gas chamber some 20 years later. How I came to be born in the Bronx Hospital, I'll never quite understand.'

As a result of his interest in the Holocaust, Milgram developed a heightened sense of his own Jewishness, and never stopped trying to comprehend what exactly had happened in Europe. He followed closely the series of military tribunals held at Nuremberg in the years after the war ended. Between 20 November 1945 and 1 October 1946, the Allied powers staged a tribunal to assess the guilt of 24 of the most prominent political and military leaders from the Third Reich. Hitler, Himmler and Goebbels had already committed suicide.

Of the 24 men, one, Martin Bormann, was tried in absentia (he was already dead but his remains weren't discovered until 1972), and another, Robert Ley, committed suicide within a week of the trial opening. Of the remaining 22 defendants, one man, Gustav Krupp von Bohlen und Halbach, was by now senile and deemed medically unfit for trial. Think of him next time you see a ThyssenKrupp product. The Krupp family history through the two world wars makes interesting reading. In the end, seven of the 24 accused men received prison sentences ranging from 10 years to life. Twelve were sentenced to death.

Many of the other Nazi war criminals who fled Germany in a bid to escape trial were tracked down in the following decades, often by Jewish survivors of the Holocaust. The most prominent of these was Simon Wiesenthal, who played a small part in the capture of Adolf Eichmann, a lieutenant colonel, in Buenos Aires on 11 May 1960.

Exactly a year later, Eichmann's trial began in Jerusalem. He faced 15 charges, including war crimes, crimes against humanity and crimes against the Jewish people. Eichmann had been responsible for many of the logistical elements of the Holocaust. In Jerusalem, his defence relied heavily on the duties imposed by military rank. He claimed that as a soldier, even a high-ranking one, a person was always responsible to somebody higher up the chain. In other words, he and other Nazis were merely following orders.

It was Eichmann's trial that gave Milgram the final nudge to put into action a behavioural experiment that he had been working on during his time at Yale. He wondered whether he could scientifically test the credibility of this Nazi defence, and in doing so come to a fuller understanding of some of the great monsters of history. His work on the subject came to be known as the 'obedience to authority' experiment.

In July 1961, just three months after Eichmann's trial, Stanley Milgram recruited 40 volunteers with the intention of answering one question: How far would ordinary people go in obeying instructions from an authority figure if those instructions involved harming another person? What the volunteers were told, however, was that the experiment would study the effects of punishment on learning ability.

The experiment, performed in a basement at Yale, is fascinating. The set-up involved three individuals: the person running the experiment, the subject of the experiment (a volunteer), and an actor pretending to be a volunteer. Between them, the three individuals were known in Milgram's mind as the Experimenter (the authority figure), the Teacher (who obeys the orders of the Experimenter), and the Learner (who was subject to the Teacher). The subject and the actor drew slips of paper supposedly to determine their roles. The process was rigged. Unknown to the volunteers, both slips said 'Teacher'. In every instance, the actor would claim to have drawn the 'Learner' slip. The volunteer subject would always assume the role of the Teacher.

The Teacher and the Learner were then separated and led into different rooms. They could communicate with each other but could not see each other. In a later version of the experiment, the actor would at this point mention to the volunteer that he had a heart condition.

The Teacher was given a list of word pairs that he had to teach the Learner to memorise. The Teacher then read the first word of each pair, suggested four possible answers, and the Learner had to try to recall the correct pairing. The Learner would press a button to indicate his response. If the answer was correct, the Teacher would move on to the next word pair. If the answer was incorrect, the Teacher would administer an electric shock to the Learner. With each successive wrong answer, the Experimenter would ask the Teacher to increase the strength of the shock by 15 volts. Before starting the experiment, each volunteer playing the role of the Teacher would be given a single 45-volt electric shock so that they would have a feeling of the punishments they would be dispensing. But the shock levels they had to administer to the Learner ran from 15 volts all the way up to 450.

The instrument for delivering the shocks was deliberately rigged to look sinister and frightening. Furthermore, the jolt levels were all labelled with tags, running from 'slight shock' or 'moderate shock' through 'very strong shock', 'intense shock' and finally the top two levels, 'danger: severe shock' and ultimately 'XXX'.

While the volunteer taking the role of the Teacher believed that, for each wrong answer, the Learner was receiving a genuine electric shock, in reality no shocks were being administered. A pre-recorded tape provided the Learner's reactions. At 75 volts, the Teacher would hear his pupil grunt. At 150 volts, the Learner would ask to be released from the experiment. There were agonised screams at 285 volts. At some point, the Learner would refuse to answer any further questions. After 330 volts there was just total silence.

The Teachers were instructed by the Experimenter to treat silence as an incorrect answer and to apply the next jolt.

If at any time the Teacher expressed a desire to stop the experiment, he was given a succession of verbal prompts by the Experimenter, in the following order:

Please continue.
The experiment requires that you continue.
It is absolutely essential that you continue.
You have no other choice, you must go on.

Some of the Teachers refused to continue the experiment at an early stage, which was what Milgram had expected. What shocked Milgram was that 65 per cent of the participants were willing to progress to the maximum voltage level. That is to say that around two-thirds of the volunteers completed the experiment, and inflicted the final massive and fatal 450-volt electric shock three times on a person that they'd only recently met on the orders of somebody that they didn't even know.

Some of the Teachers pleaded with the Learners to try harder with their answers. Some appeared to be remote from the whole experience. Others thought they had killed the Learner but still proceeded. One Teacher, who was told that the experiment must continue, kept administering the voltage while muttering to himself, 'It's got to go on, it's got to go on.'

In later modifications of the experiment, Milgram not only made the Learner visible to the Teacher but forced the Teacher to place his victim's hand on the shock plate. Milgram later allowed the Teachers to determine the level of voltage applied on their own. The average voltage was 83, and only 2.5 per cent applied the maximum of 450 volts.

Milgram concluded that most people were governed by the desire to be good and not evil but were increasingly submissive the closer they were to an authority figure. They felt more justified in pressing the button if they believed the responsibility wasn't theirs and that they were working for a reputable organisation. Personal codes of morality were over-ridden by a sense of obedience.

Milgram's findings were extraordinary, disconcerting and controversial. He shocked the world. Literally.

For some, Milgram's experiments are conclusive proof that seemingly ordinary people with regular jobs and aspirations can be motivated to kill innocent people without anything more than a series of verbal nudges from people they've never met before but who are invested with a certain authority. And in their defence it is argued that any one of these ordinary volunteers could, in theory, reasonably claim that because of a weakness in their personality, they could kill an innocent person simply because they were following orders.

If you want to be a football manager, then Milgram's experiment is mind-blowing.

I listened to the song over and over while my father regaled me with tales of Milgram's experiment and what it meant. Maybe Milgram hadn't quite explained the mentality of the architects of the Holocaust, but he had revealed something very insightful and useful about the nature of ordinary human beings.

The number 37 in the song title, by the way, stands for the number of participants in one experiment who pressed the button for maximum voltage. Peter Gabriel performed the song live for years before he recorded it. He would amuse himself by getting the audience to chant the rather spooky chorus 'we do what we're told, we do what we're told' over and over again. As a piece of performance art, it is exceptional.

One of Milgram's volunteers went on to be a conscientious objector to the Vietnam War and wrote to Milgram to thank him for having awoken his suspicion of authority. That would have been me.

I came home not knowing an awful lot more about Holland but realising two things: the importance of staying true to yourself regardless of authority; and the fact that it is possible to get almost anybody to do what you would like them to do if you approach them in the right way.

Knowing those two things just blew my mind.

You see, of all the kids who lived on my street I was the only one who was never taught how to survive.

I was taught how to escape.

The second major formative experience for me came along some eight years later, in 1996.

The mid-nineties were a micro-revolution. Labour were promising to change the UK for the better courtesy of Tony Blair. (Honestly. It's true. And we believed it.) And we even had a rich musical soundtrack to support the wave. The Gallagher brothers of Oasis were the gloriously evil kings of rock'n'roll and they had an upstart rival band of southern softies called Blur to help them prove it. Which band you preferred was a good pointer to what sort of personality you were.

It was always sunny back then. Of course it was. My friends and I were full of hope. We didn't much care for school because we loved football. Or vice versa. Everybody loved football in fact. Cynicism had yet to be invented. We all dreamed of playing for Tottenham or Arsenal. Terry Venables took England to the semi-finals of the European Championships. We exited as unlucky triers, not as laughing stocks.

Weirder still, we all got on with each other.

There was a racial divide, Indians against English. But everybody just got on with everything. We weren't being told that we had to feel compassion for people, or being forced to get on, we just did. The kids whose roots reached back into the old colonies of the subcontinent always wanted to play for Liverpool or Manchester United because historically those were England's successful clubs. Their dads had taken to life in the UK, looking for the best opportunities for success for their families, and football teams were an easy cultural anchor.

We weren't kids trekking across the vast lonely plains of social media, a landmass built on bullshit and spite. We were just kids who played out and got into scrapes together; we had fights with each other, we had laughs, and we'd forget what the fights and laughs were about almost instantly. We lived in the fresh air, the last of the species to do so.

In that school year I sat next to my best friend, Lee Stephenson. Lee was hilarious. He had a slight frame that ordinarily would have made him ripe for bullying, especially in our school, except that our clique was quite a cool group, because I was good at football and the others were good at music and, most importantly, we were generally better at being built like brick shithouses than anyone else was. Lee's idiosyncrasies were endearing; his impressions were made for TV and he deserved his own stand-up show – certainly the drama teacher thought so.

He was quick too, on the track I mean. When the school was picking its relay team to represent our shithole against the rest of the county's shitholes he was always included, alongside myself and two other friends who were also light-ning quick. We were the pride of the shithole. In fact, the boys were so quick that I could afford to take my turn on the fourth leg purely to reap the personal glory once I'd crossed the finishing line. I usually celebrated like the other three were a support band to whom I'd given a big break. That need for selfish personal glory has stayed with me. A friend asked me a while ago if I always ran straight to the guy who had given me the assist whenever I scored a goal. I could see the look of disappointment on his idealist's face when I said, 'Like fuck I did.' It was me and my adoring crowd every time.

Scoring a Premier League goal is the best orgasm you can have if you aren't sleeping with me.

Anyway, our school year swept all before it. We were like the Class of 92 at Old Trafford, except with personalities instead of money. We were sporty and could turn our hand to anything. When the posh kids from the private school across town turned up to play cricket against us, Lee would bowl bouncers at their heads and we'd intimidate them until they surrendered and we won by default. In football, forget it. We were so much better than anyone else in the county that we steamrolled the other teams. In rugby too, even though most of us didn't have a clue what we were doing or what the rules were, the two posh kids in our year would step up and do enough punching and stamping, with the rest of us joining in cheerfully, that the other school would be on the bus back across to the leafier side of town before the final whistle had even sounded.

But it was in athletics that we excelled. Lee was exceptional; he could turn his hand to any pursuit. He could sprint, steeplechase, hurdle, throw, jump – you name it and he could do it. It was remarkable. Scouts from nearby athletics clubs began to turn up at our school and try to poach him at the school gates.

For me, 1996 is still tangible. I can close my eyes and I am there – at that crossroads in my life but too happy to give a fuck which path I should take. It screams good times, an explosion of cultural significance that was felt widely and which identified with students across the county, not just in our school. It riffed freedom, possibility and youthfulness – and, above all, hope. There was a way out of the shit that had gone before, the horrible greyness and stench of death that was the 1980s. There was so much fucking giddy optimism around I'm surprised cocaine didn't become as quaint as smelling salts.

We reached a stage that year when we were either old enough to buy alcohol or had found a friendly corner-shop owner who was happy to argue with the police that we looked old enough or that our fake ID looked legit under the black light. So one day we bought a bottle of Mad Dog 20/20 and sat drinking it in the local park, thinking we were boldly going where no kids had ever gone before. Buoyed by our success with the Mad Dog, we planned a visit to the local pub. Our studiously casual approach as we hit the door and the bouncer outside it somehow worked. We got in. We were in a fucking pub. What now?

We were dressed in our best clobber, cunningly making sure that we blended in with anybody who went to a pub back then. Black school shoes, black trousers and crisp white shirts. We could not have stood out more if we'd tried.

The bar was busy, and soon enough a lively character wearing a black T-shirt, blue jeans and a pair of white trainers dutifully stepped out of the crowd to give us some harmless banter about our shirts. 'Still pressed, is it?' he asked. A few people in the bar turned to look at the first-timers and, happy to be encouraged, the man turned to Lee and said, 'Fuck me, you still got the pins in that one.'

There were laughs around the bar as everybody surveyed the group of downy-chinned tenderfoots out of their depth in new territory. We should have laughed it off, but collectively we blushed. No matter how cool and immune you might be in one world, there is always someplace else where you won't quite cut it.

We felt young and very innocent. Not the purpose of the expedition when we had planned it.

Lee put his drink on the bar and stormed out.

I felt sorry for him. He was my mate and it wasn't nice to have the piss taken out of you in front of an audience who could all remember their first time walking into a pub as an outsider. We were all dressed like clowns (well, more like waiters) and Lee had been randomly singled out from the bunch of us.

I suppose we debated whether to go after Lee, but if we all walked out the laughter would stay with us all the way home. The news would appear in the local rags, the vicar would talk about it on Sunday morning and we would be relegated locally to the Vauxhall Conference of coolness. So we stayed and played countless games of pool, feeling very conspicuous and laughing too loudly because we thought that was what people in pubs did. We were too scared to go back up to the bar to order another drink. Who would they pick off next with their crushing critiques of schoolboy fashion?

During my playing career, there were frequent moments when I'd be watching football matches from on the pitch and I knew that something I didn't want to happen was about to happen. I used to feel a flock of startled butterflies rising up in my body and in the seconds after they took flight the opposition would maybe score a goal, or a tackle would go in that severely injured one of our players, or I would push off too hard and pull a hamstring, or the referee would pull out a red card for a teammate.

That horrible ominous feeling. I have always been able to sense danger from a young age, and that talent, if you can call it that, has stayed with me. Strangely, the crowd at a game would often feel the sensation too. You've been there. You know. The crowd becomes inexplicably excited at certain moments. Something throws them into an almost blind panic and a huge roar rises up out of the belly of the stand for no apparent reason other than to petrify us players down on the pitch. We look around, alarmed, to see what it might be.

A poltergeist?

An assassination?

A unicorn on the pitch?

Robbie Savage warming up?

There was never any cause for it but it felt like a siren in your head.

And that was the feeling I had an hour later on that night. The feeling I had just before the pub door swung open and a youngish-looking man in a pressed white shirt, black trousers and black school shoes walked hurriedly towards the bar, pulled out a 12-inch kitchen knife and plunged it straight through the heart of the man wearing the black T-shirt, blue jeans and white trainers.

He killed him almost instantly.

Ah, Lee. Fuck it. Fuck it. Fuck it.

Twenty years on it makes no sense to me. It makes no sense to Lee.

You never know who you're sat next to at school. In fact, you never know who you're sat next to right now, who's downstairs or who you might meet tomorrow by chance on the tube. You never know what might drive a person to do something purely incomprehensible. Sometimes it arrives with no warning, sometimes with the mildest provocation, and sometimes the perpetrator is also a victim – of circumstance, perhaps, or of their own character.

You never know who you are sat next to. You never know what versions of yourself are locked up inside your head.

That is the part of life that no science, psychology included, can predict.

Twenty years. Twenty long fucking years later and I still can't find an answer.

I still don't know why Lee did it.

Shit.

But he did it.

And when I visit him in prison, he spends the hour that I spend looking at him looking at his own reflection in the plate-glass window. And both of us are always at a loss to explain the events of that horrific night. I know he's sorry. For him the murderer is a different person entirely, a person who no longer exists. The murderer lived and died in those few moments of madness as surely as the victim did. But Lee can't explain how he has been delivered from that person into the person he is now, lost and tragic. And until he finds the answer to that question, his parole will continue to be turned down.

That was the year my childhood died and a hardened, emotionally detached adult took the reins. It changed me and, for large chunks of the years that were to follow, I took no fucking prisoners.

Those were the two defining moments of my childhood. The day I realised that authority isn't always right. And the day I realised that what goes on in people's heads is a mystery – even to themselves. But, above all, I realised how important it is to think for yourself.

THE SECRET PSYCHOLOGIST INTERRUPTS

In a very honest way, TSF discusses two of the formative influences on his life before becoming a professional footballer. How we each react to a tragedy like Lee's is a very individual matter. I have no doubt it changed TSF's perspective on much of what followed in his own life. But I think that what TSF is speaking about more generally in this chapter is the different perspective he has always had – particularly on football.

The series of experiments that Milgram carried out gave us what we now refer to as 'man in white coat syndrome'. Anyone with the trappings of authority, we tend to follow. Imagine a policeman knocking on your door right now and saying that you have to evacuate your house immediately ...

and he can't tell you why. You just need to trust him. Most of us would do what we are told. Milgram performed many experiments to prove that we listen to and obey authority often without thinking, most of which, as TSF has recounted, resulted in quite frightening levels of compliance.

I have often thought that being a Premier League footballer is a bit like taking the king's shilling. Or a little bit like living in a communist regime. Everyone will do the same amount of work, wear the same clothes at certain times of the day, and eat the same food at the time they are told to eat it. Everything is dictated to you. Gary Speed once said to me that he hadn't had a proper Christmas in 12 years. One of the benefits of retiring was going to be spending Christmas like 'normal' people. I have no idea why Speedo didn't live to enjoy more Christmases, and my heart still aches at this tragedy.

The problem for footballers is the paradox they face. As you read this book, listen to the way TSF talks. He uses language based upon being the best: no kid at school matched his talent; have him in the side and you'll win. He talks about being headstrong and following his own path. I can tell you now that TSF reached the highest standards in the Premier League and I think at one stage would have been considered one of the best homegrown players in the league. But here's the dilemma. Many other Premier League players have the exact same mindset. They have grown up with the same view of their own talent as TSF had of his. They knew and loved the fact that they were head and shoulders above the rest. These feelings of superiority create a competitive environment, leading to 'I'm better than you and I'll show you how much I'm better' thoughts and behaviours. And while this can be a difficult environment to navigate, it helps them to achieve, to push themselves to where they want to go.

However, having fought their way up through the lower leagues, when they get to a Premier League club the rules have changed. They are no longer the big fish in a small pond. They have experienced success as an individual. But now, to succeed in a team context, they have to be compliant and follow the rules, while also expressing individuality. The message is: be yourself and express yourself with all the flair and personality which got you here in the first place; use that inflated ego, swollen from years of compliments – but make sure you drink water at this time and your piss is clear. As a Premier League player, most of your day is spent taking orders from a man with a clipboard. What weights to lift, when to get a massage, what to eat, when to practise and what to practise.

This may be a little unfair, but I am surprised that more footballers don't go off the rails. To take an example from outside football, the Nanking Massacre of 1937–8 was a tragedy of the Second Sino-Japanese War. Freed from orders, Japanese troops committed atrocities of cancerously ugly proportions; the utmost levels of barbarism. When psychologists have tried to explain this stain on Japanese history, they have unanimously agreed that an underlying reason was that the Japanese army was so prescriptive and ordered. Given the chance to operate *without* rules, they engaged in lawlessness and savagery of an unprecedented magnitude.

On a much smaller scale, I believe this is why so many players smoke and drink and no doubt indulge in other behaviours outside of hours. It is a reaction to their regimented lifestyle. But some players, like TSF, never quite obeyed the culture of authority that football demands. Discipline is important, and players know that. But balance is just as important, and players have to create a demarcation between work and acceptable play.

The perspectives learned by TSF when he was growing up – in this chapter he has described a positive experience and a bad one – are what helped make him resistant to 'white coat syndrome' as an adult. But it is not just past experiences that shape these perspectives – we can also learn to be more mindful of authority and of maintaining balance in our lives.

2. PERFORM

*Showmanship goes an awful long way
in football*

I can remember vividly the first time I met the Secret Psychologist. It was in a hotel room in Manchester on the evening before a match against Manchester City. As footballers preparing for an away game, it is sometimes the custom to follow the evening meal with a video of your opponents. Some managers do it on match day itself after a mid-morning lunch before naming the squad, in order to leave the players guessing for as long as possible. However, the players can usually tell who will start the match from the shape sessions that take place during that week's training.

Anyway, this particular evening meal was different, very different. After the last player had put down his knife and fork, the manager stood up and said, 'Don't go anywhere, lads, I want you to meet somebody who's going to come on board with us going forward.'

At the front of the room there was a table with four pieces of paper and four pencils. The lads turned their chairs towards the table and a man walked past us before standing behind the table with his hands clasped.

I should point out, I've seen so many outsiders come into a squad and tell us who they are and what they do. And every single one of them starts from the following position as far as the players are concerned: 'This is a waste of our time ... Who is this joker? ... He won't know anything about football ... We don't need him.'

Only twice have I seen anybody absolutely nail it. One was a sports scientist, at the same club actually, who used humour to devastating effect. And the second person is the Secret Psychologist. Some of the others crumbled and fell apart, which led to an instant distrust – this was not a person who could be relied on; and the others were just fucking idiots.

The Secret Psychologist chose a combination of shock and awe and humour as his icebreaker. He introduced himself first, and said that the manager had asked him to come along and have a chat with the lads because in his capacity as a psychologist he could help everyone to improve themselves both as people and professional footballers – but only if we wanted his help. A bit of swearing to give the common touch always helps a newbie on his debut and the Secret Psychologist duly obliged, though he didn't overdo it, which is critical as you don't want to appear to be trying too hard and come across as disingenuous.

The trick where footballers – and most people – are concerned is to form a common bond, an us-and-us relationship, not an us-and-them vibe. It may sound pretentious but the key is not to be pretentious. Lose the plums in your voice and communicate on the level that we communicate with each other.

He started well.

'I know what you're thinking.'

Pause.

'Another fucking mate of the manager trying to fleece the club.'

Pause. That was exactly what we were thinking.

'And you'd be right.'

Cue light but audible laughter from the players. Leaning forward slightly as a group. OK, what's next?

'I'm a psychologist and I'm very good. I've helped a lot of people. Look, I won't name-drop but Bill Gates thinks I'm God. [Pause] And so does God. But we're working on that.'

More laughter. Centre-halves wondering who the fuck Bill Gates is. Then an absolutely critical piece of information.

'You don't have to use me. You can fuck me off if you like, there is no pressure on any of you. If you don't want to talk to me or if you don't think that you need any help, then please don't worry about it. In fact, if you're playing really well and happy at home, then don't come to see me, keep doing it. Come to see me if you actually need a little help.'

Fuck me. That was gold. That was when the players in the room unfolded their arms and legs and made eye contact. It wasn't, as is so often the case when people are talking to a room of footballers, a hard sell.

He closed the deal with a demonstration.

'But, with that in mind, let me show you something really quickly, just for fun, and then you can all get back to your rooms and stop yawning.'

He told us that he needed four players to come up to the table, take a pencil and a sheet of paper and draw a picture of the manager. I sank down in my chair and folded my arms – a move that he's since told me was a critical mistake. My body language made me an easy mark.

He picked out the first player, the second player and the third, and then pointed a long finger at me.

'OK. I'm going to leave the room. I'll give you two minutes to draw a picture of the gaffer and then I'll come back in and work out which player drew which picture.'

We drew our pictures and sat down before the manager opened the door and called the psychologist back in. As he reached the table, he spun round to look at us, his hands clasped once more.

'Right. Now I'm sure you all know this – it is a fact of life that we're all different. Everyone is different. Each of us in this room is different from everyone else. But that said, some of us share similar traits; a layer of emotions and mannerisms that makes it possible for people like me to psychologically profile you and then, depending on what I find, try to help you.'

He picked up the first piece of paper and kept talking to us as he glanced briefly at it.

'For example, some people have big personalities. They are leaders. They pull others with them and put their balls on the line, and they take criticism very well because they put themselves out there, on the edge. They can deal with being shot down. This man chose to sit bolt upright in the front row as if protecting the rest of you and that's why people like him always tend to fill the whole sheet of paper when they draw things.'

And with that he scrunched up the piece of paper and tossed it at our captain, who was, sure enough, sitting in the front row. One down, three to go.

He glanced down at the next sheet of paper, hardly breaking his patter. He had us in the palm of his hand.

'Anger is a very common emotion and there are many reasons why people get angry. It can be the frustration of not being able to do something as well as you'd like. However, in the case of this person it is more likely that his anger at this particular moment is because he is not in control of doing what he wants to do, which is to get back to his room as soon as possible. He feels that somehow he was lied to when your manager sprang all of this on you at the last minute, but I asked him to do that so I could see the body language of each one of you when I walked in. People give themselves away and are much easier to read if they are in a state of surprise. Anger is a good manifestation of surprise for some people and, when I looked at this person when I first walked in, I saw that he was leaning forward in his seat, breathing heavily and genuinely looking as if he wanted to rip my fucking head off. His drawing is rushed, the lines in it are dark, indicating he has pushed down very hard, and there isn't much detail in it ... here you go, angry man.'

He scrunched up the drawing and threw it to the back of the room, where our resident hard man was sitting.

'What was it you were desperate to get back to the room for, out of interest? It wasn't to ring the kids, was it? Care to give us the title of the DVD you're so keen to watch?'

An angry reply rumbled like thunder from the back. '*The Dark Knight.*'

'Thought so. Absolutely terrible film, by the way.'

And the psychologist moved on to the third piece of paper.

'Ahhhh ... the player that everybody likes, the guy who wouldn't harm a fly. He has no enemies in the changing room and I'm willing to bet that at one time or another everybody has chosen this guy to confide in when they've had a problem around the club, because he just listens and doesn't offer any decisive opinion or advice one way or the other; he won't argue or disagree with you. And while that may make some of you feel better in the short term, it isn't a long-term solution for dealing with your problems. And that comes out in his drawing, where he's had a right go, hasn't he? Tried to make his manager look as nice as possible, tried to please him. Doesn't want to offend anybody, does he? Anyway, lovely to meet you, mate, I'm sure you're a very nice bloke judging by the way you smiled at a complete stranger when I walked into the room.'

And he threw the scrunched-up paper at the nicest player in our squad, who wouldn't hurt a fly and who everybody liked. I won't lie. I was ready to catch that scrunched-up drawing. Guy that everybody likes? I was willing to believe it was me.

But nice guys have form. Ours piped up. 'Thank you very much.'

At this point, one of the African players shouted, 'Voodoo!', and formed a cross with his index fingers for extra emphasis.

The psychologist didn't miss a beat. I wanted to join the voodoo movement. Maybe we could burn him as a witch before he moved on to dissecting my personality. As I was the last of the sketchpad four, there was no guesswork. Everybody was going to enjoy this. The spiel continued.

'Right, going well so far. Uh ... but here I see we've got one of these kinds of people in our midst. Interesting. Right, you don't get these very often but we'll make a stab at trying to unveil him. So, these people don't necessarily care what others think of them yet, on some level, they want to be noticed – but only when it suits them. These people are the most interesting people to profile psychologically because they work on a number of levels; they are multi-layered, fascinating people. Everybody is different, as I said before, but these people are different again and not always in a good way. They are selfish and they disrupt; they don't seek attention all the time because they prefer the air of suspicion around them – because that's what makes them dangerous and sets them apart, which is what they truly crave. It gives them a sense of superiority.'

It went on, painfully. Make it stop, please. The gentle breeze wafting past my ears was from teammates behind me nodding vigorously.

'This person gets a kick out of doing something out of the norm, contentious even, different, unpredictable.

Actually, these people are just plain fucking difficult at times and love planting the seeds of doubt in other people's minds simply for their own amusement. And that's the reason he sank down in his seat when I picked four of you out for this experiment at the start, and that is why he drew a picture that had nothing to do with what I asked for.'

And with that he scrunched up the piece of paper and threw it at me.

'Congratulations. You're either going to run the world one day or die penniless and alone, possibly in prison.'

There was a tsunami of cackling laughter and applause from everyone in the room. They knew, as with the three players who'd been psychologically pulled apart before me, that he'd absolutely nailed my personality in less than 30 seconds.

I didn't feel quite as intellectually superior to my teammates as I had less than a minute previously.

Do you remember the film *Good Will Hunting*? It's about a troubled and troublesome young student played by Matt Damon who has all the potential in the world and proves it sporadically by doing outrageously talented things. Yet he always seems to want to press the self-destruct button. Starved of attention perhaps?

There is one scene in the movie where Damon is sitting in the office of his counsellor, played by Robin Williams, when he spots a picture hanging on the wall. Williams has painted the picture. Damon immediately rips Williams' life to pieces by analysing how the picture is painted, whether the brushstrokes are angry or devoid of meaning and emotion, what the little boat tossed on the stormy sea represents and what Williams' state of mind must have been at the time. It all comes as an uncomfortable revelation to Williams, who doesn't appear to ever have considered what his own painting means and why he even painted it at all. Naturally, it unleashes a torrent of painful memories for Williams when it emerges that the painting was done after his wife's death from cancer. He ends up kicking Matt Damon out of his office.

That's what it felt like when the Secret Psychologist profiled me in that room. And that's what it felt like every single day of my football career. The Secret Psychologist was spot-on about me. OK, it didn't have the same emotional punch as that scene from *Good Will Hunting*, but it was an uncomfortable experience. I enjoy my sense of superiority, but I don't want to be called out on it and then held to account. That disarms me completely.

That's a secret I've never told anybody before. Up until that moment with the Secret Psychologist, it was something that I thought I had disguised in my working life. I saw myself as interesting and different. Unpredictable. That's the brand I secretly wanted for myself. Footballers wear the same strip and the same hairstyles and drive the same cars. I positioned myself away from that as much as possible and thought that I was more interesting because of it.

Then the Secret Psychologist lifted the bonnet on my brain and showed everybody that my engine was the same cc as most other people's. In 30 seconds, he made me feel like a complete and utter failure.

I couldn't even argue with any of it. That hurt. Everything he had said was true.

I can be an arsehole, just for the sake of it. I am the most Corinthian of arseholes. I do it not for personal gain but just for the love of it. I enjoy fucking up things that are supposed to go off smoothly. I like being a real-life spanner in the works. I do get a buzz from making people look stupid for my own intellectual gain, especially if I've taken a dislike to them from the outset. I like trying to prove that some people are below the station they would have us believe. I enjoy placing the banana skin in the path of the fat man with the top hat and cane. I like filtering out bullshitters. I have my little bullshit litmus test and I apply it to everybody I meet.

People I know introduce me to others with a handle-with-care warning: 'You'll have to really get to know him if you're going to get on and understand him.'

It's true.

From the moment the Secret Psychologist finished the meeting with us, he was 'in the door'. Everybody wanted to know more, everybody wanted to know how it was done, and everybody in the team worked with him going forward. Including me.

Yes, I felt like an unmasked fraud at that moment in the room, but I'm nearly as intelligent as I think I am and I reasoned that, if he could nail my character in 30 seconds flat, then the Secret Psychologist would be a good man to have on my side in any battle. Plus, if I left him alone I'd never be able to get the bastard back.

And besides, hands up anybody who isn't drawn to the idea of talking about themselves with somebody who won't interrupt with their own boring stories.

Really? Liars! Why do you think your dates never call back?

The Secret Psychologist was a hit with us because he was incredibly impressive and he was spookily accurate in his conclusions. He was confident in his subject because he was clearly an expert and, importantly, he was humorous because he'd taken the time to work out and understand his audience. He had everything that somebody trying to win over a squad of Premier League footballers needs to have in abundance; anything less and you're simply not going to get the respect or attention. In fact, very often, you won't even get past the door.

However, despite years of me bombarding him with texts asking him to tell me how he did it, he has never revealed his formula ... until now.

So, for the final time of asking, how did the Secret Psychologist correctly guess which player had drawn which picture?

THE SECRET PSYCHOLOGIST INTERRUPTS

It is interesting what TSF remembers from our first meeting. I haven't asked him before.

I think success is about self-expression. Many players in all sports 'seek to impress, more than seek to express'. If you think back to the most successful football players in the last 10 years – and I really do mean the best – I believe they have been themselves on the pitch, playing with a style reflective of their personalities. You could imagine some of the great names you're probably thinking of now playing their 90 minutes, or even their whole careers, in the same way they would have played their Friday nights.

Self-expression is not only stress-free (on this note, to prove a point, I pretended to be a vegetarian who loves ABBA, romcoms and soya milk for a good part of a year, just because the girl I was dating was hot – fuck me, that was stressful), but it also allows us to concentrate on maximising our talent. If you have to think about being – or pretending to be – someone else, you're not focusing on expressing your skills.

People who learn another language say that you often lose your personality. You concentrate so much on getting the mechanics right, you can't *be you*. The critical or conscious thinking is front of mind, and the attention is placed upon getting it right, not on authenticity or expression. This was an important lesson from my first meeting with the team. It wasn't so much about how much I knew, but about how I applied what I knew that was most important. It wasn't the content that made me part of the team, it was the personality that brought to life the content.

Having said this, some players use bravado and big person-alities to hide their feelings of inadequacy – and that's fine. We all have coping mechanisms, ways in which we deal with the situation or environment we're in. I think it's possible to

TSF PSYCHOLOGICAL TIPS: VANITY PAYS OFF

Some people like to talk about players wanting to look good all the time and devoting more attention to their appearance than anything else. And I must say that in the Euros Ronaldo did a good job of winding me up by checking himself in the giant stadium screens every chance he got and adjusting his hair accordingly. In fact, I don't think I've ever seen a player take his top off more than Ronaldo. We used to take the piss out of players who stood in front of the mirror before matches doing their hair. But consider this: elite footballers are going to be seen in the flesh by a minimum of tens of thousands of people and on the TV and extended media by countless millions.

I made that same point to my friend, the 'Nike Suit', who had a different perspective. 'We want Ronaldo to look good at all times – why wouldn't we? We want him to always look his best. After all, when you go out you put your best clothes on, do your hair and generally try to look something close to your best, don't you? Ronaldo is no different. He is on show 24 hours a day and we pay him an awful lot of money to look his best because it sells more products. It's in all our interests for him to look good on and off the pitch. You want a bigger merchandise deal as a player? Take as much pride in your appearance as Ronaldo does!'

lose the dressing room as a player, not just as a manager. But the players who talk a good game instead of playing a good game are soon found out. Showmanship that gives your talent a personality or character is fine, but showmanship that overshadows the quality of play and the outcome is another matter.

So how do we use showmanship to our advantage?

People from all walks of life cultivate a persona that maximises their talent – everyone from poker players and boxers to politicians and rock stars. It's not about being someone you're not. It's more about turning up the volume on what is already good about you. It's understanding who you are and playing to the strong points.

Here's how to do it.

It's a technique called 'act as if'. It is the psychological principle whereby you project what you want to become onto the 'now', so that you start acting the role of that person you want to be. Basically, you have to think in the present tense and imagine that you are already it.

I was working with a golfer who was ranked 200 in the world at the time. I asked him where he wanted to be and he said his aim was to break into the top 20. So I said to him, 'Imagine that you are top 20 today. Congratulations, you've made it. How would you style your hair tonight?' He refused to answer because of the ludicrousness of the question. I then asked him what drink he would order when we met in the hotel bar that evening, and what he would be wearing, what he would be talking about, and who would he talk to – on the premise that he was 20th in the world.

Moving on to the next day (the start of the tournament), I asked him what time he would get on the course tomorrow – if he was 20th in the world. How would he get his shoes out of his locker? Who would he say hello to, and who would greet him? As he started to indulge me in the game of 'act as if', he really saw himself as that player who was 20th in the world.

Interestingly, he found out two things. Normally, if there was a space on the driving range between Rory McIlroy and Tiger Woods, he wouldn't stand there and practise. He'd usually find a space with golfers who were around the same standard as him and who he knew from amateur and junior golf days. However, being a top 20 player, he would stand there alongside McIlroy and Woods. I asked him if he'd talk to them. He said, 'Yes, of course.' When I asked him what about, he said, 'The condition of the greens, course management, playing schedule, equipment.' Can you see how you don't need to be top 20 in the world to do this anyway? And can you see how your game would improve by doing so?

When I asked him what he would practise, if he was 20th in the world, it started to get interesting. He discovered through some pointed questions and some honest answers that he only practised things he was good at. (He didn't want to look bad in front of the paying public or the golfers he was going to play against). If he was 20th in the world, he could become number one! He said that he'd practise all parts of his game in order to improve and, given his top 20 ranking, wouldn't care how he looked in front of the public or his playing partners.

He ended up as 17th in the world.

This technique works if you want to be a better parent or a better centre-half or a better business manager.

The key is to ask yourself a series of 'if I was' questions depending upon the characteristic you wish to improve. Let's say I wanted to be the hardest-working centre-forward (THWCF) on the pitch every Saturday. I would ask myself the questions in the present tense. If I was THWCF, what would I be eating? What would I be practising? How would I be training? What would I be feeling, thinking, saying, doing, hearing? How would I be acting?

(In an office context, you might ask the same sort of questions if you were looking to improve a trait like collaboration. For example, if I was the most collaborative person in the office, where would I sit in this meeting? How would I listen? What would I be feeling? What would I be saying? etc.)

Choose anything you want – 'if I was the best at nicking the ball off the opposing player in midfield' or 'if I was the best at stopping my opposing number play' – and it may not give you more showmanship, but it may just add a little character to what you're doing.

3. PRESSURE

Exceeding expectations, ignoring doubters and keeping your nerve

I keep thinking of Esteban Cambiasso. Remember him? Bald. Argentinian. Great at football. At the end of the 2014–15 season Leicester City fans voted him their Player of the Year. They loved him. They couldn't believe that they'd managed to sign him in the first place.

Then, a few weeks later, when the club offered Esteban a new contract he said, 'No, thank you very much.' He left to play for Olympiacos in Greece. Olympiacos duly won the league the following season – but, then again, they'd won it 42 times before. All the other Greek clubs put together have only won the thing 37 times. So it was no big deal. Everybody had an ouzo and went home.

Back in damp old England, Leicester City were making history. They were making a revolution. They were making headlines around the world. They were making the wealthiest teams in football look like mugs. And it was great to watch.

I think I'm the only person who even remembers poor Esteban.

Last season, I watched the mighty blue bloods with the fattest bank accounts trying to figure out Leicester City. It had been 21 years since any team other than Arsenal, Chelsea, Manchester City or Manchester United won the Premier League. If you had randomly picked a daft romantic off the streets, stuck a gun to his head and forced him to pick a club outside of those four who might win a Premier League title in his lifetime, he would have blurted out the words Liverpool or Spurs. And you'd have kept the safety on.

If he had said Leicester City you would have shot him for his own good.

But it happened. And what is the framing fact of this strange season that we will tell our children?

That Leicester won the Premier League title by 10 points.

Or:

That Leicester were 5,000–1 to win the Premier League title. And they did it!!!!

No, Grandpa. You're full of shit.

Oh yes, they did.

OK, so *how* did they do it?

Spending in football usually pays off, but don't take my word for it – Deloitte, the financial people who love to study football, have the numbers to back it up. This isn't what happened at Leicester. The entire Leicester City squad cost the same as Manchester City spent acquiring Kevin De Bruyne (about £54m), and Manchester United have spent more buying players in the last 24 months than Leicester City have spent in their entire 132-year history.

That is the simplest piece of financial analysis that Deloitte has ever produced.

Leicester's manager, Claudio Ranieri, was nicknamed the 'Tinkerman' during his time at Chelsea because of his constant rotating of the squad. At Leicester, he turned out not to be a Tinkerman, but a guy who uses the resources he finds already available to him. When he arrived, Ranieri didn't do what a lot of managers do; he didn't uproot the entire back-room staff and bring his own people in so that he could feel he was in total control. Instead, he kept everybody in place, with the addition of fellow Italian Paolo Benetti, with whom he has worked since 2007. Benetti became one of three assistant managers, along with Craig Shakespeare and Steve Walsh.

Nigel Pearson (who gets too little credit for his legacy, although you can see why) had already put in place a sports science team that was quite at odds with the image of him as a straightforward drill sergeant type of manager. Ranieri kept them all and trusted them. Italian Andrea Azzalin came in to be part of that well-established group, and that was it as far as the changes went.

The effect?

Continuity. Familiarity and comfort. The players didn't arrive for pre-season to find a world of new faces and new methods to be negotiated.

The way Ranieri operated is something that has definitely caught the eye of a lot of chairmen up and down the football pyramid. And not just for footballing reasons. Continuity saves significant chunks of money by avoiding severance contracts and compensation deals, and by eliminating the expensive golden handshakes that incoming staff need if they were under contract elsewhere.

A friend of mine who owns a big, big club in England has always believed in giving his manager everything that he asks for. The problem being that, for 90 per cent of managers in the game, 'everything' is never enough. This normally flares up at just the point where the manager gets sacked.

'Well, you've given me 50 first-team players but I asked for 51. I need 51.'

Or:

'It was always going to be a difficult job. What do you expect? When I came here I noticed that we have only got 12 full-size training pitches. That's Third World. We need at least 13.'

You get the picture.

No more, though. Continuity is the new game. My friend has decided that his club will put together a stellar cast of backroom staff. Any incoming manager will be asked to mobilise that staff, who in turn will mobilise the players. No more jobs for the boys. Here is a team of sports scientists, sports psychologists, nutritionists etc. who are the best in the game. Get on with it. And his first act of continuity was to sack the manager. Well, all continuity has a starting point. In fact, he sacked him after a meeting in which the manager had been asked why the team wasn't performing up to standard and the manager's response was to question how a team could possibly perform to the highest standard if one of the TVs on the team bus is broken and the coffee machine doesn't work. It was a popular sacking.

Continuity creates dynastic tendencies after all. That's the theory anyway, and I'll be very keen to see how it works out with more abrasive and insecure characters than Claudio Ranieri.

(My favourite Ranieri story of the season is the afternoon that he and his wife, Rosanna, went to a local pub for Sunday dinner at a point when the entire city of Leicester was just beginning to dream of actually winning the Premier League. The waitress who greeted the Ranieris didn't recognise Claudio and told him that there were no tables available. 'OK, thank you,' he said, and the Ranieris were heading to their car to go someplace else when a manager came sprinting after them and promised to find a table. That's a humility seldom found in Premier League managers. Or Championship or League One or League Two ...)

Anyway, back to the football. What has been particularly admirable is Ranieri's ability to back his decisions even if he didn't know what was going to happen. He set about his re-introduction to English football with a team that played gung-ho football – they won games, but they conceded goals too, and Ranieri knew that football on those terms only ever ends up falling apart as soon as the other teams get the measure of you. What was needed was a more steely rearguard that would allow a clearly talented forward line to wreak havoc.

Tactically, Ranieri didn't make things too complicated either. He made adjustments, not wholesale changes. Ranieri used the same players in the same positions more than any other Premier League team in the 2015–16 season. So much for his Tinkerman reputation. That sense of certainty obviously pleased the guys who were playing, but there was never a whimper of complaint or a tantrum or a hasty transfer request from the rest of the squad either. Having been around the block so many times, Ranieri has reached the stage in his career as a manager where perhaps he doesn't feel the need to imitate others. He looked at the players he had inherited and made the best of them. There is a lot to be said for that when we come to consider England a bit later on.

Nigel Pearson favoured a back three. He was so close. When Ranieri realised that a European place may not be beyond the reach of the team, he tweaked the set-up of the defence. He decided that he was more comfortable with a back four. He chose four players who had a pathological fear of not being physically close to each other. When they settled into the system, they were the bedrock for all that followed. The result was astonishing. The team went from having no clean sheets in the first 11 games of the season to having 12 in their last 19 games.

Ranieri also spotted N'Golo Kanté's talent (well, listened to Steve Walsh, who had spotted it a long time before) and signed him for a whopping £5.7 million. And he generally encouraged players to do what they were good at. There were no strict orders for Riyad Mahrez, for instance. He could do what he saw fit from his starting spot out on the right wing. That made it hard for opposition teams to plan for dealing with him.

Jamie Vardy, on the other hand, runs very fast. That's the key to his game. So Ranieri manipulated circumstances so that Vardy could run very fast a lot of the time. He didn't just create space for him – he created entire prairies of space. And Vardy galloped into them like a mustang stallion.

In the past Vardy has conceded that, perhaps because he played non-league football for so long before jumping to this level, he was plagued with self-doubt. Ranieri didn't make him fit into a system; he let the system fit Vardy. Leicester's style covered large areas of the pitch. Whenever they could stretch a team with speed, they did just that. If you have teams that are coming to Leicester expecting to get something, then they are going to commit and expect to dominate possession. What Ranieri had in Vardy was an 'out ball'. Say what you will about the long ball, it can work. And it can really work if you have somebody as fast and as persistent as Vardy.

Vardy is a unique animal. He can deliver up to 500 metres of all-out sprinting in every game. In a game against West Ham early in the season, he was clocked sprinting at 35.44 km/h, a Premier League record. That was impressive in itself, but the fact that he could get close to that speed so often in a game was a unique weapon.

At one stage in the season, Leicester's long-time sports psychologist Ken Way commented that there were two psychologists working at the club, himself and Claudio Ranieri. Some of Ranieri's little touches were memorable. When Leicester let in at least one goal in every one of their first nine fixtures, he didn't hang any of his defenders from a tree on the village green. He didn't moan that Leicester just didn't have the quality. Instead, he famously promised he'd take them all out for pizza once they kept their first clean sheet.

A bunch of millionaires being brought for pizza by a genial old granddad figure?

Come on.

But it worked, because it was fun and relaxing and different. There was no stick. Just carrot. Or pizza.

Managers at other clubs would have scorned the simplicity of it. In fact, newspapers covered the pizza trip initially as a quaint eccentricity of this affable man, who hadn't really cut it at Chelsea and was perhaps trying to enjoy his swansong before being put out to pasture, probably at the end of the season. Think of what it did for the players, though. It was the perfect antidote to the plague of headphones and iPads and iPhones that isolate everybody in a modern dressing room or team bus. Everybody felt they were part of something. Ranieri knew what he was doing. As he said during the season: 'Everyone feels they are participating, so playing badly means betraying the others. They are free men, aware that they have a job and responsibility. They enjoy maintaining that.'

And the rest of us learned something else too. When we form a view of somebody based on one or two facts, we find it hard to change our opinion. When we heard that Claudio

Ranieri had brought his team en masse to Peter Pizzeria, we smiled and said to each other, 'Aw shucks, aren't old people cute? I wonder where he'll take them when they get relegated? McDonald's?'

If Mourinho had taken Chelsea to a pizza parlour (and looking back he really should have considered it) there would have been instant academic treatises on the subject, and half the clubs in England would have been belching pepperoni the following week.

We had written Ranieri off, though. Even Gary Lineker, someone I admire very much, had his own 'you can't win anything with kids' moment when he heard about Ranieri's installation as Leicester manager. He tweeted, 'Claudio Ranieri? Really?' And Lineker has genuine credibility when it comes to his history with Leicester. He's not a bandwagon-jumper. Anyway, the rest of us had the same thought. 'Ranieri? Really?'

The reaction said more about us than it did about Claudio Ranieri. Since leaving Chelsea derisively branded as the Tinkerman, he had managed with varying degrees of success: Valencia, Parma, Juventus, Roma, Internazionale, Monaco and Greece. We hadn't learned anything more about Claudio Ranieri. But Claudio Ranieri had.

During the season, there were other carrots that Ranieri dangled in front of his players. Good results equalled days off. At least the players thought that they were days off. In the eyes of the physios and sports science people, they were additional recovery days. While other teams were getting on planes to fly to European games, the Leicester players were recovering.

Something else that the days-off policy transmitted to the players was trust. Many managers are control freaks who can't let their players off the hook for more than a few hours at a time. They view management as extreme babysitting. Ranieri treated his team like they were grown-ups. So they acted like they were grown-ups. 'I make sure my players have at least two days off football each week,' he said. 'This is the pact I made with the players: "I trust you. I'll explain some football ideas to you every now and then, as long as you give me everything."'

Deal.

Not that detailed data analysis wasn't also used by the Foxes to improve the team's performance. In training sessions, all the players are monitored by means of wearable technology, providing information about their general fitness and levels of stamina. The Catapult GPS system is a pretty nifty piece of equipment that has become almost standard at football clubs. The device tracks players' speed, acceleration and deceleration. It tracks changes in direction (linear motion, and angular and rotational movements, before you ask). It's a heart-rate monitor and comes with wireless reporting to a computer within a 200-metre transmission range and a five-hour battery in case of extra time.

That's all pretty standard. What makes the Catapult the market leader is the algorithm they have added, which calculates a player's exertion based on the measurements it takes when tracking speed, motion and heart rate. This is called the 'player load'. In simple terms, the higher the number, the higher the exertion. This data gets fed back to players, to coaches and to the sports medicine staff. It provides a baseline against which each player can measure his performance and exertion.

Every week at Leicester, the players were given individual summaries of how well they had played after each match and how well they had trained. Stats included the number of tackles, the distance they covered on the pitch and other number-crunching nuggets. The player load was a key stat. Anything significantly below the baseline and you were either injured or hiding.

If that sounds like a lot of micro-management, well, it could have been so if implemented by somebody else. At Leicester it wasn't. It was useful information and fun. Stats weren't used to bully players. And the communication ran both ways. Leicester players completed a daily questionnaire on their iPads. They would be asked how they had slept, if their sleep had been disturbed; if so, there were alterations in diet and lifestyle that could be made if necessary. They would be asked how their bodies felt after the previous day's training or game. If several players made a similar complaint or comment about, say, muscle soreness or nagging hamstrings, the sports science team would adjust the next session.

Sprint scores would be presented to the group as a whole. Midweek five-a-side tables were published. Players sat together to watch clips of each other's performances.

That's always good comedy. When players are taking the piss out of each other over sprints and five-a-side leagues they aren't worrying about the same things that the players at Manchester City are worried about: *If we don't win the league, then we are failures. If we are failures, then the manager goes. If the manager goes, then there will be a clear-out. Then again, if the manager is going what's the point of me busting a gut? I'll show the new guy when he comes that my bad form was all the old guy's fault. Fucking lame-duck manager making me play bad ...*

Leicester under Ranieri built a group culture and a spirit that the players involved will find hard to match at any other club they ever join.

All season long we talked about those pre-season odds of 5,000–1 (did anybody even ask what the odds were on them not just winning the Premier League but winning it by a margin of 10 points?), but our belief in Leicester never really came down from that level. I don't know anybody who wasn't still waiting for them to collapse right up to the moment when it became a mathematical certainty that they would win.

How did Leicester handle that?

The answer is simple. They didn't. Not directly. They just ignored the pundits of doom and kept on laughing.

Ken Way, the club's respected sports psychologist, said something very interesting as the race entered the home straight – that things were so relaxed that he had taken a short holiday from work in early April. Genius. Instead of handing out valium and tranquillisers to trembling players, the club psychologist takes a few days off. The signal that sent had to be incredibly powerful: the impending crisis – what crisis?

In fact, in March, when Leicester had a down week, Ranieri told his players they were free to take off anywhere in the world. The players were sufficiently motivated not to abuse this goodwill gesture and continued to wear their monitors, so that club staff could tell they were still in peak form. The professionalism of the players is significantly at odds with that shown by a guy at my first big team, who strapped the heart-rate monitor to his dog for 15 minutes at home and was consequently reprimanded by the club and fined a week's wages after the computer showed that his active heart rate seemed to have reached 250 beats a minute at one point. Who knew dogs' heart rates were that fast? Not him.

Doubt is more infectious than confidence in football teams. In almost every dressing room I've ever experienced, there have been one or two characters who can suck the positivity out of the atmosphere in a sentence.

Yeah, what colour is the sky in your world, mate?

Yeah, I've heard it all before, mate, it was bullshit then and it's bullshit now.

You believe in that shit, then you'll believe anything, mate.

Yeah? And if my auntie had hairy balls she'd be my uncle, mate. Of course we can't fucking win it. Go back to sleep, mate, and sweet dreams.

On and on they go. Leicester didn't seem to have any of these human hoovers sucking the goodness out of the adventure.

In fact, Leicester never thought too much about long-term consequences, good or bad. They never expressed a public thought about winning the competition. They simply stayed focused on doing all of the things that they had to do. Of course there was pressure. Part of the secret of dealing with pressure is just to adapt. If you are stuck on a desert island, you can either sit down and weep and hope that a passing cruise liner spots you, rescues you and pampers you; or you can make yourself somewhere to sleep, figure out a way of finding food and develop a level of comfort with your circumstances. Leicester were always comfortable. Always confident.

Ranieri and Way recognised early on what the point of anxiety might be for their players. It was the scary nature of the gap between the present they were living in and the future they hoped for. How on earth could they get from one to the other? The answer lies in something I read years ago. Put a novice skier at the top of a mountain and he will shit himself. He's standing at the summit and he's looking at the bottom. Maximum anxiety. So stand beside him and say:

'OK, how frightening is it to ski from here to just level with that mound of snow five yards down?'

'Well, that's not so scary.'

'OK, so let's do that.'

Repeat again and again till the skier gets to the bottom.

And that's what we do in football. We break everything down until we have one cliché that actually stands up to scrutiny: 'We're just concentrating on the next game.' In our business, there is never a truer word spoken, and you might roll your eyes when you hear it but it rings as true for Leicester as it does for any other club. One game at a time – kill the anxiety.

A bitter old pro who had made the Premier League when I first started playing once told me: 'In the Premier League you'll have a run of three fixtures, and depending on how well you're doing you might think to yourself, "Hmm ... Fulham, Aston Villa and Charlton, nine points there." And if you are entering those fixtures on the back of successive defeats, you might think, "Hmm ... Fulham, Aston Villa and Charlton, we've got to win one!"'

You see how that pressure turns around suddenly? And all the while the fans are anxious, the media are ramping it up, and the atmosphere slumps. I've been on both sides of the divide. I look at fixtures like those I've just mentioned and today, with the sun shining, I think nine points. But ask me again in the dead of winter when I've sunk back into depression ...

Leicester eradicated self-doubt from the agenda. They eliminated the negative and accentuated the positive.

If you have a bad day as a player – and this is a big problem for strikers especially – the tendency is for the horror moments to linger in your head. All day Sunday you are replaying the 89th-minute chance you skied over the crossbar. Five chances you had yesterday and not one even troubled the keeper. You keep playing a lowlights reel in your head.

You go in on Monday and the gaffer says, 'What was wrong with you on Saturday, for fuck's sake?' And you don't really know so you tell him that you were just off form. And once it's put out there, once you've said it, you start to believe that this state of 'being off form' is like an atmospheric condition. You have to put up with it, like you have to put up with the weather.

The bad shit clings to your brain much more determinedly than the good stuff. There is a discipline to overriding the bad stuff and only accessing the positives. Just visualise the moments when you were king of the world. And it's not simply a question of saying that you will do it, of making a resolution to think positive thoughts – it's an environment. There has to be a positive framework around you, a happy atmosphere in the dressing room and on the pitch. If you missed five chances on Saturday, it's not helpful if the manager treats you the next week as if he has found out that you've been shagging his wife.

Leicester had that environment. They didn't catastrophise. The odd defeat was just that. No inquests. No grave post-mortems. I never had the sense that their hearts sank when they conceded a goal. I watched them play live a number of times; there was never any finger-pointing when a goal went in, no shouting, no histrionics. Just a quiet determination and a near flawless game plan that allowed them to believe that the match would still be won. Psychologists call it the Pollyanna principle.

I have a few friends playing for Leicester. Unsurprisingly, they are only too happy to talk about their success now it's in the bag. Two of them in particular had a close rapport on the pitch, and when we sat down to discuss exactly what had happened they were in unison once more.

'It was the gaffer firstly,' said mate number one. 'He took all the pressure off while making us believe that we could win. Normally, a manager takes all the pressure off and then forgets that you have to win, but he managed to do it with us.'

How?

Mate number two piped up, 'I think because he trusted us. He told us that we were all at the football club because we were good enough to be there and that he trusted us to prove that we were good enough. That's all you want, a chance to repay the manager. When a manager has trust in you, you never want to let him down.'

Very true. And the pizza thing?

Mate number one: 'Well, a lot of that is bullshit. It's not the pizza itself – which is what people have wanted to try to say. It could have been a pizza or a million pounds – the point is it's about winning.'

Mate number two: 'Yeah, that's true. How many times have you had a round robin in training [a five-a-side tournament between four teams] and the coach has pulled out five Mars bars for the team that wins the most games? You try so hard to win the tournament that in the end you forget that it was just a Mars bar that you were playing for. All you remember while you're playing is that there's a prize for winning.'

Mate number one: 'Yeah, it doesn't matter if it's Mars bars or something else. If you turn something into a competition, then it instantly becomes more attractive for players because they want to compete for anything. Every day is about competition and winning. I think it makes us want to prove ourselves: if we win the pizza, we win the competition. And then you are more confident.'

Amazing, eh? I'll tell you what's more amazing – the fact that these two clowns just pocketed half a million quid each for winning the Premier League and still insisted that we split the bill three ways. And no, we didn't have pizza.

Leicester City did something that in one sense was inevitable. They were the Bob Beamon leap in football, something record-breaking and off the charts. But eventually somebody, somewhere was going to pull off that feat. What was fascinating was how they did it. Money wasn't an equalising factor. They aren't a poor club, no Premier League club is, but they suffer competitive disadvantages in relation to the illustrious few who make *Forbes* lists and spawn worldwide branding operations. They didn't have an academy that brought forth some golden generation. They didn't have some once-in-a-generation genius who they managed to hold on to.

They had a group of players who nobody else coveted and they turned them into champions. They were fit and functional and the backroom staff kept them injury-free, but what went on in their heads was what made the difference.

THE SECRET PSYCHOLOGIST INTERRUPTS

What have we learned about football from Leicester's performance in 2015–16?

Well, reward and recognition are important for performance. But, interestingly, baubles like the Ballon d'Or may not be the ultimate motivation. Many players talk about the respect of their peers as being important. It is essential for a coach, manager or captain to find out a player's real motivation; but, to be even savvier, the best leaders of teams instil a culture that is self-policing. Claudio Ranieri's Leicester team provide a masterclass in this.

We can always use authority to drive compliance, but the best teams have a cultural commitment to doing things right. There are protocols, which in the top teams don't even have to be written down. It is a fallacy that the best teams have a strong leader. I would actually argue that some of the highest-performing teams I have worked with don't necessarily have one strong leader; they are a team of leaders.

Here is a quick example of self-policing for you. I was in South Korea with a team for a pre-season tournament. The players had to meet in the foyer of the hotel at 6 p.m. sharp in order to get a bus to the game 30 minutes away. All the players gathered in the foyer, apart from one. It got to almost 10 past and there was still no sign. The players were just mingling and chatting, or listening to their iPods, so I said to the doctor to get them on the bus and let them wait there. When the player finally showed up and was ushered on to the bus, he was greeted by a round of 'fucks' from the 20-odd guys sat with their knees pressed against their chests in a minibus with no air conditioning. It was more meaningful

69

for the team to administer the brickbats than for a doctor or coach to try to give a ticking-off.

Not that this will ever happen, but it would be an interesting exercise to allow each player to give a set bonus to one of their teammates, and for that player to decide at the end of the year whether to hand it to the teammate or not. You're probably thinking that every player would hand it to their mate. Who would do the same back. But tests have shown this not to be true. When students have been asked to mark each other's work, they have shown great peer responsibility and often marked it to the same standard as the examiner would have.

Likewise, there is a law firm that does exactly what I have suggested and hands £250 to every employee. The employees are told to give it to someone who they think has done something good that year. Instead of simply handing it to a mate, people become very possessive over the money: 70 per cent waited until the final two months to pass it over, and 32 per cent gave it to people who they didn't work with directly. The employees take their responsibility for the money very seriously, in response to having the value of their judgement recognised and acknowledged by the powers that be. Sometimes, the employer can be so far removed from the employees that they are no longer the best judge of performance.

Think about this seriously for a minute. Here's a question for you. Who in football knows the most about football? It's a general question, but if you were looking to ask someone to predict an outcome in football, then who do you think would be your best option?

The fans?

The players?

The manager?

The answer is the bookies.

Because football is a low-scoring game, the outcomes of matches may be tricky to predict – the worst team may beat the best team. Luck plays a role in the short term. However, longer predictions such as those made over a season – bearing in mind that we have just examined last year's black swan of Leicester City's Premier League win – are often more or less right.

The reason why bookies are often right is because they use the wisdom of crowds. They do not make decisions in the isolation of a boardroom. Depending on how many people believe in a possible outcome, the odds shorten or lengthen, and so they decide upon the most likely result in accordance with the views of many. For example: when Newcastle United finished fifth in the Premier League in 2011–12, the board were over the moon. So much so that they decided to hand Alan Pardew a contract of unprecedented length: eight years. However, the board clearly knew less than the footballing public. Despite the strength of that season's performance, the bookies made Newcastle favourites to be relegated the following season. In the event they finished 16th.

As James Surowiecki observed in his book *The Wisdom of Crowds*, expert forecasts are usually less accurate than the combined guesses of a crowd of people who are diverse, independent and decentralised. Based on this, you could argue that it is ridiculous that the most important decisions a business makes are almost inevitably made by a handful of people in a boardroom. The best answer to any problem would actually come from the 2,000 staff members. Or a straw poll of popular opinion. Or a focus group of fans. And so on. The aggregation of such different opinions acts as a kind of Monte Carlo analysis that gives all possible futures consideration in the calculation and produces a kind of 'expectation' or average of all possible outcomes. And so a lot of people with a little knowledge make better decisions than a few people with a lot of knowledge.

Leicester City are the black swan in this entire theory. Nassim Nicholas Taleb, the statistician who wrote a book on the black swan theory, suggested that scientific ideas can never be proven to be true, no matter how many experiments appear to support the idea. But a single contrary result can prove a theory to be false. In other words, we can say that all swans are white until such time as somebody spots a single black swan. Ranieri and Leicester were rated, by the bookies, by the wisdom of crowds, as so unlikely to win that it was nearly impossible. They were that black swan.

In years to come I think a lot of us will look back on Leicester's achievement and the take-away will be how they held their nerve when everybody was expecting them to implode. What they did in winning the Premier League while bigger, richer clubs fell away was a metaphor for how every player and every team should deal with the problem of nerves. I have a checklist for the problem. There is no big-picture solution; you cope with nerves and anxiety on a day-to-day basis.

DEALING WITH NERVES

1. *Acceptance.* It's OK to be nervous. Expect it and accept it. In fact, there are some athletes who will tell you that they're more concerned before an event if they *don't* feel nervous. Anything you feel is right. You are always on your own side. Anxiety can actually be a facilitative emotion if you don't let it get the better of you. Another thing to accept is that you probably won't sleep well the night before your game, if that's your thing. Don't worry about it. Worrying about it only makes you feel worse – you don't sleep and you don't like yourself for it. You end up feeling bad about feeling bad!

2. *Reframe the butterflies.* The extra adrenaline in your body that kicks in when you ignite your fight-or-flight response triggers a whole host of physiological reactions, one of which is that feeling of butterflies in your stomach. Perceiving your physiological symptoms as 'bad' means that when you feel butterflies you will inevitably label yourself as being nervous. Changing your perception of those butterflies can help with your nerves. When you start to feel anxious on match day, reframe the butterflies by telling yourself that you're not nervous, that your body is simply becoming excited and getting you ready to play.

Reframing in general is an excellent aid to performance. The classic reframing example – seeing the glass half full, not half empty – may be simple and overused but it has its merits. How we speak about things determines how they make us feel. So be careful of your words, they shape your actions. Choose to speak about things in a way that will aid performance.

3. *Give yourself an emotional boost.* Your emotions play a very big role in your behaviour. Your emotional state will alter your feelings of motivation and confidence as well as govern how much effort you put in. You 'feel' your emotions because there are different physiological changes associated with different emotions, and those physiological changes can either boost or dampen your physical performance.

One recent study showed that outcomes were significantly enhanced for sprinters when the athletes imagined a very happy moment in their lives immediately before their race. Give yourself an emotional boost by thinking about your best performance. But it doesn't always have to be about visualising success; it can be your favourite scene from a funny movie, or any happy memory from your past, or thoughts of your kids that make you smile, laugh and feel good.

4. *Stop comparing.* Are you looking around at your rivals and feeling like you don't stack up? Are you worried about how you're going to perform compared to the people around you? Comparing yourself to your teammates and competitors can fill you with anxiety. The problem with success is that we see it as comparative. We measure ourselves against people who

are the same age as us, or who live in the same street, or who went to school with us. This is wrong. Success is the continued journey towards goals that are personal to the individual. We can only measure success by how much we are fulfilling our own potential. You need to gauge your success based on *your* goals and *your* performance, regardless of what anyone else around you does. It's your day, it's your game. Don't compare game to game either. Even if the conditions are similar, every match day is different. You need to trust yourself, trust your training, and just focus on your own play and your own journey towards being better.

5. *Stay in the moment.* This is one of the most important and impactful things you can do to alleviate your anxiety and improve your performance – and one of the hardest. Keep your mind in the present moment. Stop time-travelling into the past, fretting about the training you think you should have done. Stop travelling into the future, worrying about the outcome of the day. As human beings we do it all the time. Even when we're lying by the pool on holiday, we love to be thinking about the restaurant we went to last night or about the bar we are going to tonight. Instead, we should just be enjoying that moment on the lounger at the water's edge. Stay right here in the conversation of the game and you'll be more likely to adjust and adapt to the challenges and demands that come. Breathe, stay in the moment, and enjoy the day.

4. BEHIND THE SCENES

Why your manager threatened to stab you

If you really want to go into management, then you need to give it your heart and soul. There is no other way – unless you just want to survive one job, engineer a quick payoff, pocket a handy million or two and then disappear. This happens more often than you would think. Players with big names to trade on see a short managerial career as a means of topping up their retirement fund by a seven-figure sum. Off the top of my head, I can think of at least two without really trying.

I've played under the full variety of managers. Every different personality type. And they have always interested me. A manager is exposed to the behavioural and emotional fluctuations of a large group of players. He has to deal with the same fluctuations among his staff. And he has an internal life. He feels good, he feels bad, relations are happy at home and bad with the club owner, or vice versa. Some managers consciously use psychology to deal with and manipulate these situations. Others wouldn't know the difference between psychology and physiology, but without knowing it they are handling psychological situations every day of the week.

Managers can be good tactically or they can be good technically. Neither of those strengths is enough on its own. The coaches and analytics team will come up with a game plan most of the time and very often you, the player, will never even see it. Your job is just to execute it. Your job is to carry out the instruction, not to question it. That's where the psychological relationship between the manager and his players comes in.

I have learned the things that I wanted to learn from the managers I played under. I don't remember the advice that didn't resonate with me; I remember the lessons that did strike a chord. The psychology that I saw working. Nine-tenths of that was about how managers dealt with their players away from the pitch, the part of football the season-ticket holder never gets to see. The information we very often try to keep under wraps. So here are my top tips for behind-the-scenes management.

1. DISCIPLINE

The best managers hot-wire discipline into their team. There are two ways of doing this. The first is to show that you are a disciplinarian by making an example of a player the first time he goes off the reservation, even if he's a good player. Sir Alex Ferguson was the master. Any player who pissed him off was gone. Gone. Big name, small name, some as big as your head. It didn't matter to Sir Alex. Just as I wouldn't let a teammate switch off and fuck up my chances of winning the game, Sir Alex wouldn't allow any ego or personality to fuck up his chances of immortality. He was ruthless, utterly ruthless. He shoved David Beckham out of the door and to this day Beckham still calls Sir Alex a father figure.

Dave, your father rejected you, very publicly too! Did you not notice this?

The second way to instil discipline is to earn respect. There are managers out there who are less feisty in the dressing room than Sir Alex. They couldn't switch on the so-called hairdryer treatment to save their lives. But they have earned respect. They solve problems emphatically and in their own way. The best manager I ever had was soft-spoken, methodical and strategic. But he'd had a wonderful career and he was fair. If you earned the right to keep your shirt, then you kept it no matter who you were playing next. He didn't believe in swapping players around to give the side the best possible chance of winning the next match. He was consistent and he delivered.

He believed that the players who were in form would have the best chance of winning the match. Sounds obvious, right? Wrong. Eighty per cent of managers do not agree with that approach. They are sometimes hoist by their own petard when the chairman tells them, 'You asked for 40 players, right? Well, why the fuck aren't you using 40 players?' The manager feels the pressure and guesses that he has no choice but to start fielding players that he doesn't really want to play. I've seen it happen so often. Eventually it dooms them. Always.

Life is easier for a respected manager.

You trust him.

You listen to him.

You run through walls for a living but for him you will run through the walls leading with your face.

And that is reciprocal. It has to be. The same manager will appreciate that a talented player isn't always influencing every minute of play, but he trusts him to execute that one little piece of magic that might open up a stubborn back four. So he leaves him on the pitch until the last minute. For the first few games, the player might not be sure. He isn't playing well, so why isn't he being whipped off? Finally, he scores or sets a teammate up with an outrageous assist and it clicks. 'The manager trusts me.' And when that trust and mutual confidence spreads through the team, you can be greater than the sum of your parts.

I've played under both styles of management and they both work, providing you have players who respond to each method. When a manager recruits players, he needs to pay attention to personality as much as to physique and playing skills. A relentlessly negative player will suck the soul out of your team. A rebellious player can make a manager look small. Don't sign what you can't handle.

I remember playing for one manager in particular who ruled by respect rather than fear. We were on a pre-season tour, playing in a tournament in Asia as a Premier League side. You generally tread water when playing pre-season games and that's why some results appear skewed at times. So our team might be playing at 50 per cent energy levels while the opposition are generally as fit as they'll ever be. But the players were working hard and carrying out the manager's instructions to the letter where possible. He understood that occasionally we would make mistakes, but so long as we handled them in the right way the situation could be retrieved and normal service resumed.

Just before a big game against a massive South American club, I was sitting on the bed in my hotel room watching the TV, waiting until we were due to get on the bus and depart for the stadium, when I made the fatal mistake of closing my eyes. I was woken by an angry phone call. As I struggled to get myself awake, the world fell out of my eyes. Footballers have recurring dreams. Nightmares. In the way that you might dream about being naked at work, our recurring nightmare is that we arrive at the stadium for a match and the game has already kicked off. Every footballer has that dream. I've had it more times than I care to remember.

The assistant manager said, 'Where are you?' and I replied, 'Oh fuck, sorry, I fell asleep.' Very quietly he said, 'We're on the bus waiting to go – hurry up.' I felt sick; it is a horrible, horrible feeling, especially when it's not expected from you. I shot down in the lift, out the door and on to the bus, where a very angry-looking set of management staff were waiting for me. I raced past them to my seat towards the back and the players just looked at me. Some smiled. They knew I was fucked.

We lost the game. I think it is the most angry and frustrated I've ever felt after a match. Maybe. In the heat and humidity, I'd lost a stone in weight during the game. I climbed on to the bus, sat down, took out my phone and saw that it had no signal. I was so angry that I pressed my thumbs into the screen until it snapped and then smashed it to pieces on the corner of a chair. No phone for the rest of the tournament.

The worst part was that I knew I had to talk to the manager at some point, but there never seemed to be a good moment. It was a restless night, partly because I'd fallen asleep earlier, which had done nothing for the jet lag and my circadian rhythm. The next morning we were driven to the training ground, put on our boots at the side of the pitch, and wandered on to the field to knock some balls about. The management team ambled out and the coaches called the players into the centre circle.

Unusual.

Shit. I knew what was coming. So did everybody else. I was about to be hanged.

'Listen,' said the manager to the players huddled around him, 'we're in a foreign country, things are different and as a result we may do things differently as individuals, things we wouldn't do back home. But we still have to accept responsibility; after all, that's what a team is. If you let down your teammates, or us, then you have to own up to that mistake with an apology and not run away from it. If you don't, it means that you have no respect for your teammates and no respect for us. And that's not on.'

That was the way of that particular manager when he was angry. Low-key and disappointed. I felt like shit. It hurt more than any wild rant would have.

He dispersed the players while I walked towards him. He grinned. That's how he was. He'd let you stew in your own shit just to make his point.

'I'm sorry, gaffer, I fell asleep in the hotel room. I was all ready to go and I must have just closed my eyes for a second. I'm sorry, gaffer.'

'Apology accepted,' he said. 'Try not to do it again. Everybody will make a mistake, and I expect everybody to own up to it and everybody will be treated the same. Even you.'

I was never late for another training session, match, public appearance or private chat ever again. He taught me a valuable lesson by humbling me in the process.

In contrast, I worked with another manager who ruled by a 'one strike and you're out' policy. Unless he needed us again a few months later for his own purposes, in which case he would climb down. This manager loved to do shape work on the training pitch. In fact, that was all he did. Shape work is mind-numbing but essential. It involves standing as an 11 on the pitch, with the manager throwing a ball into various areas and watching how the team react. They should get into the position required to best defend or attack, depending on where the ball is. We were generally in the right place, but he'd come around each one of us and move us maybe a yard to the left or right; he'd move me about a foot back or a foot forward. We felt like Subbuteo players. It was infuriating. Imagine a game going on at full pace and you're looking around to see if you're a foot too far forward in the face of a moving ball. Ridiculous.

But it was the way he moved us that pissed the players off. He literally grabbed these grown men by their upper arm, like a kid being hauled out of a sweet shop by his dad. Some players let him get on with it. Some of us tried to pre-empt where he'd move us to.

Personally, I hated it.

As time went on, we began to crack smiles at each other after he'd moved us and we'd roll our eyes as if to say, 'Is this guy for real?' He sensed it, no doubt about it. What respect we had for him was seeping away. One day we had someone injured and a reserve player came in to take his place for the weekend's match. He was out on the left wing and he hadn't tucked in as far as he should have. The manager duly grabbed the player's arm and tugged him towards the middle of the pitch.

'Leave it out,' said the player, 'I can move there on my own.'

'OK,' said the manager. And he shouted to the side of the pitch where three other players were jogging up and down to keep warm.

'Come here,' he yelled at one of them. 'Take his place on the left, will you?'

And he sent the other player off the pitch. He never played for us again. It was precisely the opportunity the manager had been waiting for. He just needed somebody to question his authority in the slightest way before making a real example of him. It was utterly ruthless, very difficult to watch and humiliating. We're talking about players who had won Premier League titles, been top scorers at clubs, won trophies and international caps all over the world. They had played with some of the game's greatest exponents. And they were being manhandled by this fool who thought he was zealously policing a march by some students.

Here's a strange thing that tells you a lot about football, though. It worked. Two things happened. The player never played for us again. And nobody ever said a word on the training pitch again.

Key psychological point from the Yorkshire school: there's nowt as queer as folk.

2. DIPLOMACY

The key to a squad of players performing well is harmony. Oddly, though, that harmony is brought about by things that look decidedly inharmonious.

Competition, for example. Competition is a great motivator, providing there isn't much to choose between all the players in terms of talent. But competition can lead the more emotional players to the brink of argument. Some rows are defused very quickly. Others rumble on. A manager needs to be sensitive, or his technique may damage the team cohesion that he is hoping for.

The problem should always be dealt with once it has been spotted, but not immediately. A lot of events in football are sparked by emotion and ego. Very rarely can they be sorted out on the spot, when people are still mad. There is too much risk of loss of face for all parties. In a reasonable timeframe, though, these things should be dealt with.

When there is a fight on the training pitch, for example, the only solution is to send both players in, with one of the coaches to keep them apart. You can't have two players continue training after they've come to blows. Legs would get broken. Sending them in is for their own protection. Fights almost always happen during the small-sided matches, as these are the height of competition as far as training goes. The flashpoint generally occurs when one player on the losing team, who has had enough of this shit, puts in a bad challenge to make his point. He usually chooses to tackle the player on the winning team who is doing most of the goading.

It is hard to describe what it's like being on the losing side of a five-a-side match. It's different to losing a proper match on a Saturday, when it feels as if the world has come to an end. I think players look forward to the five-a-side at the end of training so much that it takes on a kind of winner-takes-all magnitude. It becomes the point to the week, the competitive element that has been lacking up to Friday morning. And we like the bragging rights that go with a win; we like teasing and goading the losers. It's a chance to rub it in, to prick the egos of mates. We like providing our own bits of commentary when things are going well: 'Oooh, the veteran has totally done the young full-back. Still has it.'

All fun and games till somebody loses an eye. Or bruises their ego. Or gets nutmegged. I've seen a lot of hell breaking loose after a nutmeg. Good managers spot the moment when a losing team throws in the towel and the winning team starts to showboat. That's when it's time to blow the whistle. Failure to do so will generally render your squad smaller by one come Saturday.

Small-sided games usually start in a jovial manner because everybody is looking forward to playing in them. There might be an occasional nutmeg with an accompanying cackle, and everybody else laughs. It's still 0–0 so it's funny. When the score is at 5–0, the problems start. The same nutmeg is not met with a laugh or a smart comeback. It's met with a very late tackle. Lots of players accept that and let it go. But some call the offender out.

And that is exactly what happened when our midfielder and our left-back, who were close mates off the pitch, decided they'd both go in for a tackle. The midfielder played the ball, the left-back arrived the following Tuesday having taken the scenic route. His tackle didn't involve the ball – the only contact he made was with the flesh between his friend's foot and his knee. He ran his foot right up the shin. Everybody winced. They both jumped up, squared up to each other and, before we knew what was happening, the midfielder had head-butted the left-back clean on the bridge of the nose.

What the fuck?

They were immediately sent in to cool down, accompanied by one of our coaches. The five-a-side was promptly ended and the squad was sent home.

The midfielder arrived the following day looking grim and serious. The left-back arrived with two enormous black eyes. His appearance was like an advert for fisticuffs. People asked questions. Unfortunately, the media had got hold of some details. (Not from me, I hasten to add. I wasn't in the business of leaking stuff to the press at this point.) It was a Thursday. Media day. This is when players are put forward by the club's internal media staff to field the press's questions about the game coming up on the Saturday.

The manager called us all into the centre circle before training. Our manager was very good at speaking to the broader group while really addressing his comments to the one or two players who needed to hear his point. This morning, though, he was faced with a situation that needed direct intervention. If not, there was the potential for it to continue and maybe escalate.

'We're all competitive,' he said. 'We all want to win and sometimes things can boil over. Everybody understands that; we've all been there, I think. It's OK for us to have arguments, but we must never become more physical on our own training pitch than we're prepared to be on a Saturday in the face of the enemy. If you're being more physical here, then it means you are not giving enough on a Saturday.'

Good point.

Then he told the left-back and the midfielder that he wanted to see them. After training. He was a manager who would make players sit in their shit until he was ready to deal with it. What followed was a masterclass in diplomacy. The media knew something had happened but they had no details. All they knew was that there had been an incident between two players at the training ground. Our manager made both of them sit in the press conference and field questions, with the threat of a £2,000 fine hanging over each of their heads.

Bang. First question. 'How did you get those black eyes?'

Ball in the face from this idiot next to me.

Second question. 'Were you aiming for him?'

I'm not that good a shot. If I was, I'd ask the gaffer if I could play up front.

Third question. 'So there were no fisticuffs or coming together as has been rumoured?'

Nah. We're best mates. We shout at each other on the pitch but we've never come to blows. In fact, I think one of the biggest strengths in the squad is that we're so together. All our anger and determination is centred on the opposition.

By the time the press conference finished the pair were laughing and joking and normal service was resumed. They were in cahoots, pulling one over on the media. And they were getting away with it.

They were as happy as two pigs in shit.

The manager hadn't even gone into the media room. He was so confident of his strategy that he didn't need to oversee it. He sat in the canteen with the rest of us. When the two emerged 20 minutes later, he asked how they'd got on.

'No problems, gaffer,' said the left-back. 'But I've told them I've handed in a transfer request for being made to do the media.'

Laughter.

And that is how you deal with a problem like the one above.

What you don't do is what another of my managers did at my very first professional club when two players had an almost identical scrap on the training pitch. He fined them and banned them from the squad for two weeks. During those two weeks, the squad lost three games. The short-term decision to fine the players and pocket the cash backfired badly. The added tension sparked a terrible run that saw us finish outside the playoffs. We had been in contention for automatic promotion at one point.

There were other problems that season but I really feel – and I know some of my former teammates do too – that the incident and how it was dealt with had a significant role to play in costing the manager and his staff their jobs.

I sometimes wonder what that manager spent the £500 on. Lawyers maybe?

3. COMMUNICATION

Years ago, at my first club, we had a manager who everybody labelled with the same word: crazy. Looking back now, I think that he was ahead of the curve.

Nowadays in football, when you retire there is a tendency to look back on everything through rose-tinted glasses. Nothing in your life will be as vivid or as emotional as your playing days, so your hindsight isn't perfect. I'm sure, though, that this man was on to something back then. It was just that British football wasn't quite sure what.

He was one of the first managers from Britain to travel to Italy of his own accord. Specifically, he headed to Juventus, to see how they did things. What he found was a team that was ordered and disciplined in everything it did. They ate the right foods, did the right exercises, carried out the manager's instructions on the pitch to the letter and never questioned anything. And always together. But more than that, they had weapons. They had creatine – a powder that, when mixed with water, magically restored the energy in the body's muscles.

I was told by the older professionals not to like the manager. He was different, he was dangerous, he was liable to fly off the handle. But I did quite like him and he taught me some lessons that stayed with me: always be on time (unless you accidentally fall asleep due to jet lag); never question the manager's authority (after fining me for doing just that live on the radio); and always give your maximum and practise, practise, practise as if your life depends on it. Great lessons.

He picked on me a little bit, but only because he saw my potential. He got his message across to me plain and simple. This is your big chance; listen to me and you'll make it. I did listen and I did make it. (Actually, he used to scream at me on the training pitch in front of everybody, 'Well done – that's why you'll be a millionaire!' Which was both incredibly seductive and embarrassing, and didn't endear me to any of the jaded older professionals.) And he knew that others around me would try to get their claws in; maybe they were jealous, like the players in their mid-twenties who were in the process of missing the boat, or maybe they were bitter, like the old Scot who openly hated my naivety and scorned me every chance he got. Or maybe they just didn't spot the potential and only saw another kid who could be abused.

And that was the assistant manager. He didn't see what I was capable of. He didn't see the point of me or my presence. Actually, he didn't want to see it. He shouted at me, called me out, picked on me in front of the older pros and, being a gym nut himself as a legacy of terribly injured knees from a very ordinary playing career, he made me lift weights. All the lifting directly injured me and caused me problems for years after.

I think the manager must have noticed. And he saw that I needed help. The creatine was reserved for the older players, who needed to recover faster, and I was probably still seen as a kid who should have had all the energy in the world.

TSF PSYCHOLOGICAL TIPS: YOU MIGHT BE INJURED BUT THAT DOESN'T MEAN YOU CAN'T HAVE FUN

Reverse psychology is a great thing when it's used to wind somebody up for nothing more than banter. Whenever I'd get knocked out on the pitch, which was quite often, the physio would run on and ask me how many fingers he was holding up. I'd always tell him the wrong number. Eleven. And in a perverse kind of way, that's how he knew that I was OK.

But I wasn't an ordinary footballer who had come through the youth team. I had come into football late and from the real world. This was all new to me. I wasn't used to the workload of hardened professionals and it was telling.

This manager taught me that salvation can come from the least likely place. A player can be enthused by the slightest thing. Every now and again the manager shows that he's on your side. And it is a beautiful thing because it doesn't happen so often and rarely in front of an audience.

The manager and his assistant had been working together for years. They were tight. The manager got a job and the assistant always went with him. Usual story. They'd actually enjoyed a bit of success, a couple of lower-league promotions. But that isn't to say that they always agreed.

After training, we were sat in the changing room, having been debriefed on how pre-season was going and how we were looking forward to the season ahead. Then, in front of the entire squad, the manager turned to me, a kid, and said, 'How are you feeling?'

Everybody looked at me. Why him? Why is he suddenly so special? Nobody glared more than the assistant manager. His eyes burned holes in me.

I told the manager that my legs were heavy but I was enjoying it nonetheless. It was my first pre-season. First rule: As a naive kid always say that you are enjoying everything. Your teammates will laugh at you, but there is no comeback to a kid who says he's enjoying it.

'OK,' said the manager. He turned to his assistant and asked, 'Have you got any creatine here?'

The assistant manager didn't take his eyes off me. 'There is some in the boot of my car,' he said.

'Good. Can you get it for me and give it to TSF, please?'

'When?'

'Now, please.'

'There's no rush. I'll get it for him tomorrow.'

The manager took a step forward and turned to his assistant. He seemed to have been waiting for a chance to assert his authority.

'Am I talking in Norwegian?' he asked. 'GO AND GET THE FUCKING CREATINE NOW ... PLEASE!'

Holy shit!

The whole changing room seemed to shake. Twenty-five footballers jumped out of their skin. The assistant took his eyes off me and turned to look at the manager, who had his gaze firmly fixed on him. He thought better of making any protest and just walked out of the changing room. Five minutes later, he returned with a huge tub of creatine and handed it to me.

'Here you go, mate, two scoops with a pint of water after training.'

I remember it as though it was yesterday. I think I grew a foot taller.

I now realise that my manager was communicating with everybody in that dressing room all at once by asking one simple question: Do any of you have a problem with this guy? Because I don't.

The rest of the squad, the bitter Scot, the mid-twenty-something losers and the steroid head that was our assistant manager, they all backed off. They had been warned indirectly to lay off me. And one of them, the most senior figure apart from the manager, had been used as the sacrificial lamb. If he could be tarred and feathered, then they all could too.

Why communicate with one player if you can, with a single point, transmit your message to a whole squad? It's very clever. Maybe his assistant manager was beginning to get above his station; maybe some of the older pros – who he wanted to move on – were annoying him; and maybe I just needed a final push to come into the limelight for the club. He thought about all the different aspects of what needed fixing and nailed them all in a 10-second outburst.

I ran through walls for that manager thereafter. I didn't have to fear anybody. He had my back and he also knew that I had the type of personality that meant I wouldn't let him down.

That, and the creatine, made me unstoppable for a time.

4. AWARENESS AND INTUITION

There was a kid at our place. You see them come and go. This one was pretty unremarkable. He didn't look the part and he didn't stand out too much either. Also, he was quiet. Really quiet. We'd signed him from a lower-league team that had a great reputation for turning out exciting youngsters. Most of us thought that this time they had sold us a pup.

For the best part of a season he slipped under the radar. He was there but not there. He was picked as last resort for small-sided games. He wasn't a name. He wasn't fun to have on your team.

Our club was big, very big. We were gunning for promotion and doing well. We'd topped the table for a large chunk of the campaign and were favourites to go up. Then came the wobble. The wobble that every single club in the history of football has when the winning post is in sight. Apart from Leicester City, obviously.

But even during the wobble, nobody ever considered that a kid might be the answer. Except the manager. The manager saw something that we couldn't see. We were a team that kept things very tight, worked hard and nicked big games 1–0 or 2–1. As a team that plays that way, the moment you stop scoring is the moment the defence starts to panic. Strikers have to give defenders something to defend, and the defenders have to reassure the strikers that the 90th minute is as good as the first minute to score a winner. It's simple. A delicate balancing act beautifully in sync.

But the drought went on; the tension found its way into the stands, and the team became nervous. Something wasn't right and the manager sensed it. For the next home game, there was an unfamiliar name in the starting 11.

It took the kid 25 minutes to score. In the next game he scored again, and in the game after that.

The manager's gut feeling was right. It wasn't desperation that made him turn to the kid, although it may sound like it. No manager at a big club is desperate enough to call up a kid like this. You have to know. And our manager knew. He'd been watching him in training when we weren't. He'd seen the kid practising after hours when all the rest of us could see was the inside of a hotel room and some shit TV programme.

Soon we were rising once more, back into the playoffs, looking ominous. The bookies had us as favourites again. We'd uncovered a gem and, when a big club adds that to its arsenal at the right time, it's usually game over.

In his 10th game, with the opposition on the ropes, I played a pass to our boy wonder. He ran on to it and I waited for the net to swell. Instead, a defender interrupted his path to goal by rupturing the kid's cruciate ligament.

And with the kid's career went our hopes of promotion.

The same gut feeling that had afforded the kid his chance now served to tell us that this was not going to be our season. There is something about certain players lying in a crumpled heap on the floor. You know what has just happened to the team. Some players carry the hopes of an entire club at certain moments. Even kids.

We lost in the playoffs. Our gut had told us we would.

But I learned a valuable lesson from that manager. Desperate managers often make poor decisions. This was different. He'd seen something that everybody else had missed. It was intuition backed by a lifetime of expertise. He could have been a hero now. But instead he's just another manager who failed to achieve promotion. Those are the margins in professional football; they really are that tight.

Some managers think they have the intuition when they don't have anything to back it up. How many times have I seen a young player, who has been on fire in training but who doesn't normally start, suddenly get the call to save the club? A dozen? Easily. I've yet to see one work out. It will be a player who has performed above his usual level over the course of the week. It will be deep into the season and the players who have 35 games under their belt, playing twice a week, will be sparing themselves in training. So this guy suddenly looks 50 per cent better than he did last week.

And when Saturday comes, he stinks the place out and a big hook appears and drags him off the pitch early in the second half. His confidence vanishes and, when we think of him, we remember that time when he was king of the world in training but didn't want to know in the bitter, unforgiving cold of Goodison Park. Not his fault. Just poor management.

Managers can get confused. Some people call it being too clever for their own good. I just call it being confused. Confusion and desperation can be terminal for a manager. As players, we watched for the symptoms and shook our heads when we saw them.

I played in a team once in a playoff semi-final. The winner would play at Wembley for the right to compete in the Premier League the following season. We had played with a stringent 4–4–2 all season and it had served us well. On our day, we could cause anybody problems.

The stadium was sold out, the city was buzzing. This was our moment. But there was a surprise when we got to the ground. The players parked their cars and walked through the hordes, through the players' entrance and into the bowels of the stadium. In the changing room, there was a flipchart with the team written on it underneath the cover. We never lifted it up; we always waited for the manager to come in and reveal the team.

He did that. What was beneath the cover was a fucking shock to say the least. The team was set up as a 4–3–3, with two youth-team players filling the wide positions in the offensive three. I honestly thought it was a joke. We had international players in the squad and seasoned pros who were champing at the bit to play.

One of our midfielders punctuated the silence with, 'What??'

I was more shocked than most. I wasn't playing. Any pro worth his salt believes that not playing him is a major mistake.

This was crazy. Players worth many millions of pounds sat on their arses wondering what the manager was doing. Having got the team here in the first place, just as they were about to get a part of the glory that football so rarely affords, it was snatched away. Deliberately. It didn't make any sense.

The game kicked off and we had our pants pulled down. In small-sided games, when a team wins 5–0 we say that the losing team has been 'tampered with' and we implore anybody who will listen to 'call the police' because 'there's been a murder' – always said in a Scottish accent. Think Taggart.

That night our city was tampered with but the police never came.

Instead, the chairman came for our manager. The two lads who started, fresh out of the youth team, lasted 30 minutes. It was such a shame for the great man to end his tenure that way. But he lost it. Totally and utterly lost it. His awareness and intuition deserted him and desperation and foolhardiness rushed in.

Gut feeling has a backbone. It has substance. There are mitigating circumstances and stats that back up the decision to play somebody who wouldn't ordinarily get a look-in. Desperate managers try to manufacture such moments, but it is those managers who are able to keep their eye on the prize in the face of external, and sometimes internal, pressures who are generally rewarded.

5. ACCOUNTABILITY

Sir Alex Ferguson was the master of accountability.

A United defeat was always somebody else's fault when Sir Alex spoke to the media. The referee didn't play enough added time. The pitch was awful. The fixture list doesn't favour United. We always have tough matches straight after Champions League games. The opposition didn't play football and kicked our players instead.

All of these examples have one thing in common: not once did Sir Alex ever blame his own players. Ever. Inside that changing room, they will have had strips torn off them if they hadn't performed, but publicly Sir Alex never hanged his own players. Never. He took accountability for defeats by protecting his players from criticism and steering the media towards a scapegoat. And like idiots the media lapped it up. They did Sir Alex's work by applying a little pressure on refs or the FA, who hate being talked down in the media. That's how Fergie Time was born, that extended period of injury time that was granted to United when they were in trouble.

Sports editors would commission their in-house illustrator to come up with some graph or pie chart to show whether or not United were playing less injury time than their rivals, or had more injuries as a squad, or had had more penalties against them or red cards. And that took the place of the two extra paragraphs in the match report that should have been given over to asking why United had actually played badly.

It's tough to be a manager if you keep criticising your own players. I can recall Mick McCarthy's stint at Wolves, where every post-match press conference was met with the same answer: 'We're not good enough, simple as that.' Imagine being a player in that dressing room, being told every week that you aren't good enough and then being asked to go out and face Chelsea, Tottenham, Liverpool and the rest. Crazy. I don't even admire the honesty.

Accountability comes in many forms. I admire the Sir Alex style of accountability. Not many managers have the self-awareness to see the benefits.

I played for one manager in the lower leagues who used football in the same way that a school bully uses the class weakling. The game was a means of distracting him from his own sense of worthlessness. He was jealous of the fact that every player in the changing room earned more than he did. Every single week he'd shout at us, asking if we were just there for the money.

No manager asks his players this. What are you supposed to answer?

He had put together a team of names in the belief that football is played on paper. When it didn't work, he came to resent the money that these players were earning from the very contracts that he'd put in front of us. And it ate away at him. It all came to a head at half-time during a game against Derby. We were debagged at Pride Park that afternoon and the manager had lost it.

'You earn twice as much as these fuckers,' he yelled, 'but they care 10 times more than you!'

It was bullshit. We were just a poor team. Full of names all right, but winding down. It wasn't that we didn't care as much; it was that we simply couldn't get back the hunger that goes with having nothing, and nothing to lose as a result. In relation to us, the Derby players had nothing but they played as a team. As individuals, we would have thrived in other teams, but not all together.

The manager singled me out. 'You've been fucking shit.' And so on. 'What the fuck am I supposed to do? I've tried everything with you lot.'

OK, I'll tell you what you can try. But you're not gonna like it …

'Gaffer,' I said, 'what if we actually spent time on the training pitch in the week and, instead of playing five-a-sides every day, we actually worked on shape and how we're going to play? I think this is the first club I've been at where nobody knows how we're supposed to be playing.'

Well, that particular incident ended in a stand-up face to face, with the rest of the players pulling us apart.

But I was serious. Up until then, we had never been out on to the training pitch and gone through our shape play, and that was because the manager had put together a bunch of names that he wanted to be part of, and he wanted to please, and who he fully expected would simply take care of business. But football doesn't work like that. He didn't want to do any of the boring stuff. He wanted to be like us. And you can't do that as a manager. Give a footballer an inch and he'll take your wife. It's just a fact, I'm afraid. (In fact, that works the other way around too. There is a current Premier League manager who has slept with more of his players' wives than most players I know. And that's going some.)

The whole sorry relationship ended in the car park of our stadium a few months later with the same manager threatening to stab me. Where did those happy days go, I wonder?

I'm writing books and doing other things. I don't think he is working in motivational psychology. Pity. It might have helped him figure out where it all went wrong.

THE SECRET PSYCHOLOGIST INTERRUPTS

I'm sure that many managers down through the years have wanted to stab TSF. That's understandable, but probably not the long-term solution.

A manager should not look to push a player, but rather to pull a player towards him. The best managers, those who enjoy long-term success, ensure that they drive commitment, not compliance. When we use authority or force, it can yield some short-term action, but it doesn't create sustainable change.

Managers always try to change the way players act, but the precursor to our actions is our thoughts. We can tell people to be different all we like, but does it make much difference? We tell ourselves all the time to give up smoking, drink less, exercise more (but enough about me) – but do we do it? If it doesn't work on ourselves, why do we expect it to work on others?

It's not about changing behaviours, it's about changing thoughts. The problem in football is that managers tend to have a more traditional view of ... well ... management. They like to drive compliance and adopt a style mostly based around telling and directing.

Managers who seem to enjoy more support have a way of pulling players towards them. They are magnetic. This does not necessarily mean they have a big personality, like Mourinho, for example; this is not about charisma, it's about honourable intentions and integrity. This is about an ability to create real rapport and even likeability. The key weapons in the armoury of a 'pull' manager (Steve Bruce, Owen Coyle, David Moyes, Sam Allardyce, Garry Monk) as opposed to a 'push' manager (Gary Megson, Billy Davies, Tony Pulis, Mark Hughes, Neil Warnock) are understanding, humour, fairness, personableness, open-mindedness. They are team players.

An analogy from business is the strategy used by Virgin. It positions itself as a brand that is the people's champion. They take on the big boys on our behalf; they will fight for us against British Airways and Coca-Cola, and as a result we love those cheeky chappies and the mischievous, playful way they take our side. The 'pull' manager does this. He finds a way to maintain authority, while also having the players' best interests at heart. He is likeable because he is one of the team (and generally wears a tracksuit instead of a suit).

If you want to get the most out of a player, make them want to play for you. And this starts with your thought process, not your actions. People who you manage understand that if your intentions are right, nothing is wrong. Players should want to turn up and perform because they see you as part of the team just as much as someone who leads one.

5. THE TEAM

Working with them and for them

When I retired from football, I thought for a while that management was for suckers. The smart boys went to where the smart money was. They became agents. I was a smart boy. I decided to become an agent. I cleared out the box room because we would need the space to store all the easy cash.

Soon I had a handful of young players on my books. Or on my phone, actually. One was highly promising, the rest were pretty good. One highly promising player is enough for a budding agent, though. I would network. I would put together a DVD of his golden moments. (Not really, we don't do that anymore.) I would look after the kid as if he was my own brother. I had given him tons of advice and help when we played together late in my career. He knew that I cared about what happened to him. I wasn't just his Mister 10 Per Cent.

What I came to realise pretty quickly with my fledgling agency was that, between the playtime of the transfer-window periods, 90 per cent of my time was being spent dealing with players who were just having a bad day. And it doesn't take much for a player to be having a bad day. For example, if the player has lost a five-a-side in training and been picked on by the coach because it gave the coach some pleasure to see a promising player getting more and more wound up during a harmless match, well, then I'd get a call. I would take that call. You can't not take your client's call.

There were many other flies in the ointment of a player's happiness. Put on the B team in a training game. *WTF?* Being asked to room with somebody else. *Why me?* Scored three in training and the gaffer never said a word. *Does he hate me?* Free boots arrived from footwear sponsor but with some other player's name on them. *Why do Nike/Adidas/ Puma disrespect me like this?* (This happened to one of my players; I swear he nearly cried.)

So the phone call would come in and the player at the other end of the line would be up on a high ledge with a police helicopter circling and a list of demands. Very emotional.

I'm not in the team.
That player/coach is a total cunt.
The gaffer keeps picking on me. Seriously. He hates me.

All these upsets led to the same conclusion: the player needed to leave his club. He would never turn from a pretty handsome duckling into a great majestic swan while he was being pecked at by all these know-nothing crows.

'Fuck this club, I want to leave. I *need* to leave.'

So an hour of the day would be spent going through (ta-da!) the Five Point Plan. The Five Point Plan was a little psychological trick I picked up from my own agent. He was the best in the business, and I knew from personal experience of having shouting matches fizzle out into light banter that it would work every time.

STEP ONE

Don't say a word until the player realises that he is the only one talking. About then he becomes self-conscious and wonders if the line has gone dead. Just wait for the moment when the player says, 'Hello? Are you still there?' in a somewhat pathetic, slightly embarrassed little voice. It's a tiny bit sad and a big bit funny, but it really draws the sting out of his opening rant.

STEP TWO

Water down your empathy with a healthy dose of perspective. Leave a moment to give the impression that you are thinking and then start a story which begins with the words: 'I remember when ...' Be as creative as you like here. A little shared experience goes a long way in teaching a player that there is nothing new in heaven or earth. For example, 'You know, I remember when something really bad happened to me as a player. Not taking away from what happened to you today, but this was miles worse. I'd come in on the Tuesday morning after scoring three against Villa ...'

Deliver it in a steady tone that suggests all the way through the tale of your torment that it all worked out OK in the end. That's very important. This approach works well with dodgy media stories about the player – 'tomorrow's chip paper and all that'. By the time you have finished there should be no need to say, 'Come on, for fuck's sake, it's not that bad.'

STEP THREE

Talk down the offending party. Diss him. It might be the coach or another player or the dinner lady, but mention that they have form. There've been a couple of altercations in the past at other clubs, where he picked on players or he was mouthy in games or she gave a player peas when he wanted carrots. And then pivot. Point out that respected managers and coaches in the game (all good friends of yours) have good things to say about the offending party. In fact, when he's not being a total cock, you've heard that he actually has very positive things to say in private about your player.

Wait a second.

'Really? Yeah? What does he say?'

Players love to hear good things about themselves. Soon your client will believe that the manager/other player/dinner lady is only being an arsehole for the sake of your client. Cruel to be kind.

STEP FOUR

Give him a piece of information that you would never normally volunteer and perform a big name-drop in the process. This draws the attention away from the issue at hand and leads the player into a discussion that might offer up juicy bits of gossip.

For example: 'I had dinner with José Mourinho's agent on Tuesday. You will not believe what he told me about Wayne Rooney ...'

Or:

'Actually, talking about you going to Manchester United reminds me that Mourinho told me something very weird the other day about Pep Guardiola. Have you heard this? Don't know if I'm the first to hear it or the last but best to keep it to yourself just in case ...'

STEP FIVE

Finally, having safely defused the player, you reassure him. Thank him for bringing the matter to your attention and tell him not to worry because you will be having a word or two with somebody quite important. Never give the name of an actual person because football is a tiny, insular world where everyone knows everyone else. And now close the deal by offering an incentive. This is very important. You must always end a conversation of this nature on a positive. It's good for everybody. 'Listen, I wasn't going to say this but Liverpool are watching you next week.' Or the far more common, 'Are you all right for boots?' The answer is always yes, and what this does is plant the seed in the player's head that he doesn't actually want for anything in his life and that, by extension, you must be doing a great job.

And that's how you win at being an agent 90 per cent of the time. That's the tradecraft. The trouble is that it fucking wears you down. Most of the time I just wanted to scream, 'Shut the fuck up, you baby! What do you want me to do about it?' But you can't do that because the art of being an agent is, basically, diplomacy for babysitters.

When I think about it now, the players were just being players. It is infuriating when a coach is laughing at you and picking on you in training. It does ruin your week when you get so frustrated during a session that you and another player have a blazing row and come to blows. And there is absolutely no doubt that the worst thing in the world for a footballer is losing a football match on the Saturday. Add an own goal or a red card or some other howler into the mix, then it genuinely feels as if suicide is the only answer when you get back to your house in the evening.

Post-trauma, there is only one man to pick on in that situation, one man who can talk you down from the roof, after you've told him you want to burn your house down with your family in it and then emigrate: your agent. But for the agent it's draining, and what I soon realised was that I couldn't deal with footballers on this level; I just couldn't deal with people like me.

So why are footballers, who usually only work in the mornings, playing and training with mates, who receive masses of adulation and wheelbarrows of cash, not as easy to deal with as, say, nurses, who are generally underpaid and overworked but very cheerful? Why do teams who qualify for

World Cups, the stuff of their dreams, often disintegrate into a squabbling rabble or an ineffective mess? Hello to France, Holland and England at this point. Why does a Gus Caesar or an Adnan Januzaj show every sign of 'making it' and then stall. How can a Leicester City bolt from the pack and come out well clear at the top of a long Premier League season, while the clubs with better and more expensive players and marquee managers toil behind them?

The answer in most cases is psychology.

As petals go, we footballers are no more delicate than the rest of you, but the environment we grow up in is wildly different. For a start, the notion of 'self-esteem' is just a first cousin to the concept of 'self-confidence', which in itself is a cousin of 'sports confidence', which is what most footballers have. We are sports confident. That doesn't translate into anything else except money.

We have played for long enough and well enough to have mastered the skills. We have trained hard physically and mentally. Hopefully, within the organisation we play for we have some effective leadership – that always helps. And we have a sense of comfort in our working environment. Yes, we strut a bit and we beat our chests and wave our fists and do little dance moves when we score or when we win. We are greatly rewarded and widely adored. And deep down most of us fear that somebody, somewhere, is conspiring to take us out of this surreal situation.

So we make phone calls to our agents whenever something goes wrong because they are paid to understand us.

All that most of us have to rely on to get us through a highly pressured environment is that sports confidence. Usually, we have grown up in dressing rooms and on training grounds. That is a narrow, very male-dominated world compared to most people's experience. We have been meeting expectations in this very narrow world since we were maybe eight or nine years old. We've sacrificed things like gap years and universities. We are ignorant of the motives and mechanics of the world around us. We are designed exclusively for our environment, and we are scared shitless that somebody is going to evict us from it.

For that reason, I'll always be glad that I came into football late. Having been able to navigate in the real world meant that I never took football as seriously as some did. And what my dad taught me about Stanley Milgram and the electric shocks left me with a lifelong suspicion of authority, which stood me in good stead. In fact, the world I came into reminded me in some ways of another famous study, the Stanford Prison Experiment, which (small world) was conducted by a high-school friend of Milgram's, a guy called Philip Zimbardo.

Zimbardo recruited 24 sane and stable individuals to volunteer for a project. The plan was to divide them up arbitrarily into two groups, 'prisoners' and 'guards', for a two-week period and to monitor how the environment and the allocated roles altered their behaviour.

At first, the prisoners didn't treat the guards with any level of seriousness or respect. They made fun of the guards as they tried to cling on to their own sense of worth. So the guards began to show their authority by subjecting the prisoners to physical and mental punishment. By day two, there was anarchy. Prisoners refused to wear uniforms and barricaded themselves into their cells. Guards used fire extinguishers on the prisoners.

When order was restored, the guards stripped inmates of their clothes, destroyed their bedding and put some into solitary confinement. They began rewarding certain prisoners for good behaviour. One prisoner became so unstable by the end of day two that he had to be released and replaced with another volunteer who had been on standby.

Things got so bad that Zimbardo had to abandon the experiment after six days. The participants – students – had fallen into their roles with a greater enthusiasm than expected: the guards became cruel, the prisoners became passive and depressed. By day six, one prisoner was on hunger strike and fellow prisoners were turning on him. Zimbardo concluded that 'situations can have a more powerful influence over our behaviour than most people appreciate, and few people recognise'.

I'm not saying that the life of a professional footballer is in any way comparable to the life of a prisoner. Then again, the lives of the volunteers pretending to be guards and prisoners in a basement in Stanford weren't all that comparable either. The point is that in stressful environments we all fall into patterns of behaviour. Players who earn maybe 10 times as much as a manager always defer to him as 'boss' or 'gaffer'. Managers deal with players who they feel threaten their authority by throwing them into solitary confinement – sorry, I meant to say by throwing them into youth-team training sessions. Long-term troublemakers are transferred to another institution. Good, compliant behaviour is rewarded. Questioning the institution is discouraged.

It's a narrow world with high walls around it. Different rules apply within those walls. If your friend retires and becomes the manager, Kenny Dalglish-style, from day one you stop calling him Kenny and start calling him boss. You conform. When José Mourinho shouted at Dr Eva Carneiro nobody in football was surprised except her. If you work in a coalmine you expect dust. If you work in a pressurised, emotive, stressful world like top-level football you expect to get shouted at. People live with it.

So footballers drive big cars and date or bed flashy women; they mimic each other and they mimic the players who have gone immediately before them. As a fairly homogenous group, we struggle to remind the world that we are all individuals. And we are reluctant to test out the limits of our individuality beyond wearing brightly coloured boots or sporting a mohawk haircut. Dealing with us, dealing with each of us, is one long, never-ending behavioural experiment.

All that is why putting a good team together is more than a Noah's Ark exercise (two strikers, two centre-halves, two full-backs, two wingers etc.). It's why the oligarchs and tycoons won't always win. The ark that Claudio Ranieri filled up at Leicester wasn't full of prime examples of each species.

The endlessly quoted pre-season odds of 5,000–1 confirm that. Bookies are wrong as rarely as I am.

But Leicester, when they escaped relegation the previous season, had finished with a strong run of results. Sure, they finished at the wrong end of the table, but in sports science there is a theory put forward by a guy with the quite fitting name of Richard Lazarus: 'positive denial'. This is where you slightly distort your reality in a positive direction. Leicester had finished that season strongly and they started the new season with a few more good results. It was a positive environment, and in the right environment players who had hardly entered our consciousness turned into giants.

Wes Morgan? Last seen on loan at Kidderminster Harriers before he joined Leicester. He should have been fading from the scene, not heroically captaining Premier League champions. N'Golo Kanté? One season in Ligue 1 with Caen? Who? Suddenly, in the spring of 2016 France wanted him, having never picked him for a single underage team, and he went on to be part of their whole European Championship adventure. His first competitive international was the opening game of the championships. Riyad Mahrez? The best thing on his CV was six goals in 60 games with Le Havre in Ligue 2 before he came to Leicester. He finished the 2016 season as PFA Players' Player of the Year. We could go on and on.

By contrast ... I have always been a Spurs fan. We talked about winning the championship from maybe Christmas onwards. The history. The glory, glory days. We were back.

We just had to wait for Leicester to fall apart. In the end, it was our team that buckled under the weight of it all and finally exploded into small pieces, against Chelsea of all people. In hindsight, it was a great season, but it ended without the trophy and with slipping from second place to third. Arsenal took the second-place slot that we had considered our rightful consolation. That hurt. But I'd predicted it on Twitter as early as February. I know football. I know Spurs. I know Arsenal. If we had finished the year by storming from seventh place to third we would have been wildly happy. But this?

Being a footballer is very simple. Practise – not till you get it right but till you can't get it wrong. Expose yourself to situations. Harden yourself to the environment. Sit on the bench long enough so that the ebb and flow of the crowd noise means nothing to you anymore. Imagine yourself out there. Visualise it. Go out there and do it. If you fail, do it again. If you keep failing, change your environment – ask your agent to get you a move to a lower-level club because nobody in this dump understands you.

On the other hand, it is endlessly complex. You aren't just a digit in a profit-and-loss account. You are trying to perform in an environment where so much of what happens is random and instinctive, even for the teams who do the most planning. And the expectations in this environment are ludi-crous. Football is a world where hindsight has an absurdly high value. Defeat is a disaster. Two back-to-back defeats is an epic catastrophe. Winning is everything, and people think that is incentive enough for a player. But there are a thousand little motivation points working within any team and those complex group dynamics.

Really, you don't secretly hope that the guy who took your place today doesn't get a two-week layoff-style injury or a red card or make some sort of mistake that has the gaffer shaking his head? Honestly, you don't want to score more than your striking partner? So you really don't ball-watch because you don't trust your centre-half partner and you like to be seen bailing him out? You're a goalie and you genuinely don't reserve your most special abuse for the full-back who thinks he is something of an artist? Or the manager is for the high jump – do you all really care about what he says or thinks anymore? Come on.

Let me tell you about motivation within a team environment. Let me tell you the most cutting thing that any teammate can say to another. Once it is said, you will do anything to have it unsaid. It doesn't involve swearing; it doesn't involve criticism of your looks or your family or that girl you were with. It is seven words that make the blood boil because when they're said they're absolutely true. And they sum you up.

Every footballer reading this will recognise the following scenario because it has happened to every single one of us at some point in our careers.

You go away from home to any other Premier League club and you get 'bopped', as we call it. After 70 minutes you're 3–0 down. There is no hope and the situation has changed from one where you are trying to get back into the game to one where the best you can hope for is not to concede another goal. Things are bad and you feel shit. Personally, it feels as if you haven't touched the ball all game. Who is to blame for that? Everybody else, of course. Selfish, incompetent bastards.

In your head, you are working out exactly what you are going to say to the manager after the game when he calls the players out in the changing room. It is too much to deal with; you get angrier and angrier. Eventually, you totally toss off the last 20 minutes of the game. You don't try. You don't run. You do the bare minimum.

You're sulking. We call it 'spitting your dummy out'. Everybody can see you doing it but that's kind of the point. You care so much that you don't care anymore is the muddled message you are sending out. Basically, you are letting everyone down, but you're past caring at that point because you're angry and feeling sorry for yourself. It's a toxic combination of emotions. Afterwards, it will be referred to by others as 'head-loss'.

On the coach on the way home (and it is a hell of a long way home) you're desperate for somebody to come up to you and say, 'Hey, today wasn't your fault, don't worry about it. It was those guys at the back of the bus – they're the ones who lost it for us today.' But nobody ever says that. Paranoia sets in. You can't hear what they are saying (maybe because you have your headphones on and are staring out of the window) but you imagine everybody is talking about you. You shut your eyes and try to sleep, but the supplements and sugar drinks and gels mean you're more awake and alert than Keith Moon on speed.

The next day is Sunday and you spend it at home slowly coming out of a depression about the game. You watch the live Sunday game and hope that somebody else gets bopped. You check your phone every 10 minutes to see if anybody has texted you to say that the whole team is sorry, that they understand. Nothing.

Eventually, you have a couple of glasses of wine and slowly you begin to feel that the world isn't such a bad place after all. You take a soak in the hot tub maybe and think to yourself, 'Tomorrow I'm gonna fucking show everyone how good I am. I'm gonna get on the ball and train hard and next week against Southampton things will be different. I'll fucking drag the whole team with me.'

So Monday morning comes around and you step out on to the training pitch. The players are in huddles, obviously still talking about Saturday's game or about your head falling off, but you're blinkered to it. You don't care. You are focused on training well because you want them all to see that if they'd given you the ball more often on Saturday things might have been different for them all.

But the lads have other ideas. On Saturday they couldn't give you the ball because the team was swamped by the opposition. (Maybe we had set the team up in the wrong formation and just got soundly beaten for that reason – it can happen.) So this morning when training starts and the ball comes to a teammate and he absolutely should pass it to you, everyone knows he absolutely should pass to you, he ignores you.

Why? They can all tell that you are up for training this morning. And even if you weren't, the pass to you was the right one to play. And if you mislaid your head on a Saturday when everybody else forgot to pack their balls, shouldn't the others bring you back into a state of confidence?

No. He hits it 40 yards out of play, pretending he's trying to find the opposite wide man. He's making a point. You scream at him because you aren't the team's sulk-in-residence anymore. 'Hey, fucking pass it in here? For once?'

And then he utters those seven words that every single player has been desperate to say to you that morning; but he's the first to get the chance and he loves it.

'You want to play now, do you?'

Honestly, as I write those seven words, my stomach turns to knots. It is the single worst thing that any teammate can ever say to you because it actually crystallises all of your most paranoid thoughts. It holds up all the issues that you've been trying to push to the back of your mind for two days. On Saturday afternoon, in front of 60,000 people and a TV audience and your teammates, you tossed it off and you left them holding their dicks. And you had hoped that nobody noticed. You had hoped that maybe somebody saw what a complex being you are and understood you.

But they did notice and the simple verdict on your little sulk isn't complex at all. If you are going to get back into the group, you are going to have to earn it. You might be funny and smart and sceptical about things we don't question, but when the chips were down you turned your back. You were one of us at three o'clock on Saturday. By five o'clock you were somebody we can no longer rely upon.

You are a selfish prick.

As the ball is retrieved, you look around for some support. Shit, you've had laughs with these fellas. You've played through mud and sleet and shit and you have won and lost together. Surely one of them will give you a small smile or roll their eyes or wink? Some little gesture that just says, 'Don't worry about it.' But this morning you are the sinner who has gate-crashed a conference of the saints. Even your closest allies (so you thought) in the squad offer nothing. The guys who seemed to be part of your group, the gang with the inside track and the healthy cynicism? Your friends? Nothing.

Nobody is going to back you up because you are toxic and contagious. You know what you did on Saturday, don't you? And then you catch the eye of the manager. Surely he will intervene to stop this mad descent into barbarism? It's his team, for fuck's sake. He makes eye contact with you just long enough to raise his eyebrows before looking away. One gesture that expresses his thoughts perfectly: 'Well, what the fuck did you expect this morning?'

Trust me on this: there is no lower place in football than finding yourself ostracised by your teammates because of your own actions. I have been depressed playing football, I have grieved over losses and mistakes, but that sense of isolation is the worst feeling that any player can have in their career. You could lose the World Cup final on penalties and it wouldn't be a patch on how bad it feels when a teammate says, 'You want to play now, do you?'

I've been in that position and it has taken me up to four games to win back my place. I sat on the bench and learned a valuable lesson. I knew that when I retired I would always look back with regret on how I cost myself four whole games of my career because I sulked for the last 20 minutes of a football match. Careers are short and retirements are long, and I knew that among the things my teammates were talking about whenever my name came up was the day I lost my head and spat out my dummy. An indelible stain.

Eventually, of course, if you are a decent enough player you are brought back into the fold at the point where the punishment is starting to hurt the team instead of you.

You do everything to show the world how good you are. You run hard for your teammates and the fans and for the old lady you met in Sainsbury's who asked you to reach the last Canderel off the top shelf. You bust your gut to prove your worth. At the end of the game you win but nobody thanks you, nobody says well done, because they know and you know that that is the minimum requirement for playing professional football – and you sure as hell better never forget it again.

And when it is all over and you become a manager or a coach or an agent, the first thing to remember is that the people you are dealing with are the sort of people you once were.

Not a very pleasant thought, but hugely useful.

THE SECRET PSYCHOLOGIST INTERRUPTS

I once worked with a player who was a high-performing inter-national. And he knew it – he knew what it was that enabled him to score goals match after match. But what made him so brilliant individually were also the characteristics that made him an unsuccessful team player. When he left the club, he was the star player. The other players were quietly devastated. He left in the January transfer window for a top-four club and European football. He also left us one spot off relegation.

I decided to do a presentation to the players. I drew a vertical line straight down the middle of the whiteboard. I said, 'OK, lads, on the left is what this player gave us. On the right is what he didn't ... Who wants to start?'

Someone shouted out, 'Goals!' I put the word 'goals' on the left. 'What else?' I asked quickly. Someone immediately came back with, 'He didn't track back.' I duly scribbled it on the right-hand side of the board. 'Didn't stop the diagonal' was the next one, followed in quick succession by 'not a team player', 'won't work hard when up against it' and several other critical comments. It got to the stage where the only thing in the left-hand column was goals, and there were at least 10 things on the right. The game ended when one of the players volunteered loudly from the back, 'He was pretty shit when you think about it!' and laughter broke out.

The truth is, this player was not shit. He was brilliant. I didn't carry out this exercise with his teammates to do him a disservice or belittle him. I did it to try to build them up after what was perceived as a real and palpable blow. The interesting thing was that all the items in that right-hand column were tasks that he could do. He just chose not to. His reluctance to do those things certainly didn't come from a lack of technical ability; it came from not possessing a character which had the team at its heart.

To be part of a team, we have to be ourselves, but we also need to be aware of what I call reflective behaviours – how our behaviour impacts the group. And, seeing as success cannot take place in isolation, the best players will get the most out of themselves by being true to their character, but also get the most out of their teammates by realising which areas of their personality create a strong team dynamic for a winning performance.

We cannot make an unrealistic shift in personality, nor should we try. It is about looking at the different personality traits that we already possess. I sometimes think we should be quite binary about this. It should be easy to question in a simple yes-or-no way which aspects of our personality contribute to a better team. It is important to be a winner, but just as important to be a winner who creates other winners.

We need to see the commonality in ourselves and others: what are the characteristics we have within us that allow us to play well and create better performances in others?

6. LEADERSHIP

The manager's guide to mind control

Eighty per cent of management is psychology. Some people in the game think that it's 90 per cent and others 70 per cent. Anybody who thinks the figure is less than that isn't worth listening to.

I have asked almost everybody I know in football to what extent their manager uses psychology as a percentage of his overall job. The results were interesting. Those who had played for Sir Alex Ferguson all felt that his job was made up of 10 per cent coaching, 10 per cent picking the team and 80 per cent managing people and situations. One player I know at Chelsea told me Mourinho was 90 per cent about managing players on a day-to-day basis and that he rarely coaches. Wenger came in at 70 per cent, but that was from a scout I know at Arsenal, not a player, and Claudio Ranieri was also 70 per cent, as he likes to get involved on the training pitch.

The point is that the job of a manager is like the job of a chief executive at a corporate monster. He doesn't make the products, he doesn't do the advertising or the marketing and he doesn't cook the dinner at lunchtime. But he oils all the cogs. If a problem crops up in any one of those areas, then he is ultimately responsible, and that means he needs excellent psychological skills in terms of his communication and his ability to resolve multiple issues. He can't please everyone all of the time – the idea is to keep most of the people happy most of the time.

In his book *Misbehaving*, Richard Thaler talks briefly about football – American football that is, not real football. Nonetheless, the lessons are the same: people who manage are an odd breed. Thaler is a professor of behavioural science at the University of Chicago and has spent a lifetime studying the irrationality of the world around us. Sport is an interesting area to delve into if you are interested in irrationality. In one study, Thaler and an assistant researched player selection in the NFL to see how the NFL draft was affected by irrational bias. In other words, with millions on the line, how do managers in pro sports choose their players?

Once a year in late spring, the NFL stages a draft during which teams select prospective players. Every team gets seven picks, and the whole event – the players entering the draft as well as the needs of the NFL teams – has become a media spectacle. The draft gets shown live. Entire magazines and websites are devoted to predicting who will end up where.

The draft works on a weirdly democratic basis. The team with the worst record in the previous season gets the first pick. The team that won the Super Bowl in the previous year gets the last pick. There are seven rounds in the draft so everybody gets seven picks. The kink is that teams can trade their picks to other teams. If you have the right to pick fourth, you might agree to give that up for two picks in later rounds. Teams can also trade picks this year for picks in future years.

When Thaler began his study he had the feeling that teams placed too high a value on the right to pick early in the draft. He told a story about a guy who was a local hero in Chicago, having played for and coached the Bears at various times in his career: Mike Ditka.

Ditka was in charge of the New Orleans Saints in 1999 when he committed professional hara-kiri. After two losing seasons, Ditka decided that the one thing that would make everything better was if he could sign Ricky Williams, a Heisman Trophy-winning running back from the University of Texas. Ditka announced this to the world at large. He, Mike Ditka, was going to go out and fetch Ricky Williams down to New Orleans.

The New Orleans Saints had number 12 pick in the draft that year. Ditka was worried that Williams might have been snapped up by another club by then, so he put the word out that he would be willing to trade all of his picks for the 1999 draft if he could get Ricky Williams. Not a smart thing to do. So Ditka traded all his picks to the Washington Redskins, who had the fifth pick in the draft, at which stage Williams was still available. But Ditka didn't just give Washington his 1999 picks; he threw in the first- and third-round picks for the 2000 draft as well. By the end of the 1999 season, New Orleans (even with Ricky Williams) were ranked second bottom, so they ended up giving away two very high picks for the 2000 draft, which would have guaranteed them top players.

Ricky Williams, as it transpired, turned out to be pretty decent, but he didn't transform the New Orleans Saints. To make matters worse, after the deal was done and Williams had come to New Orleans, Ditka agreed to pose with Williams for the cover of *ESPN* magazine. It was no ordinary photo: Ditka appeared in full dress suit with white carnation, and poor Williams stood beside him in a white wedding dress, solemnly clutching a bouquet of flowers. The headline read 'For Better or For Worse'. And the next season was worse. Ditka, now a laughing stock, was fired. New Orleans went without all the decent players they might have had.

The general findings of the study that Thaler performed were as follows:

- When Thaler put all the players in any given position into the order by which they were picked in the draft, he figured that if teams knew as much as they thought they did, then the third-picked player would always be better than the fourth-picked player, the fourth better than the fifth, etc.
- If the teams had zero ability in picking, then 50 per cent of the time the third-picked player would turn out to be better than the fourth pick – the same odds as in flipping a coin. By applying a series of performance-related criteria over the following seasons, Thaler analysed 400 picks right across the draft and discovered that teams

had on average a 52 per cent record in choosing whether or not one player was better than another. In the first round, where they were concentrating super-hard, the figure was a bit higher, at 56 per cent.

Every manager thinks he can tell the difference between a potential star and a potential bust. If you follow the prices extracted for high-value picks in the NFL draft, then the first player picked should be five times better than the 33rd player picked. They never are. Ever.

The conclusions Thaler came to about the psychology of head coaches seems to me to be very applicable to management in the Premier League:

PEOPLE ARE OVERCONFIDENT

They feel that their ability to discriminate between the talents of two players is greater than it is. We've all been at clubs where the expensive new favourite purchased by the manager is an obvious dud. Everybody can see it except the man who paid millions for him. He in turn may have fallen victim to people making forecasts that are overblown: scouts are too willing to say that this player or that player will be a superstar.

Pick your own fabulously expensive transfer flop and apply lesson accordingly.

THE WINNER'S CURSE

When several bidders compete for something, the winner is often the bidder who most overvalues the object being sold. The same is true for players wanted by management. Take José Mourinho and Paul Pogba as an example worth watching. Lots of other teams liked Ricky Williams. Nobody liked him as much as Mike Ditka did. Mike Ditka never coached again.

THE FALSE CONSENSUS EFFECT

People tend to think that other people share their preferences. An example Thaler gives is that those who own iPhones think that everybody has them. In the draft or transfer market, when a manager falls in love with a player he thinks that everybody else has fallen in love with the same player. Step forward Seth Johnson. In fact, all of Leeds United circa 2002.

I've heard so many stories over the years of managers overlooking failed medicals because they thought they'd got their hands on the player everybody wanted.

PRESENT BIAS

Owners, managers, coaches etc. all want to win *now*. For the players selected at the top of the NFL draft, there is always the illusion that they can turn a losing team into a winning team. The same applies to transfer-deadline-day signings. A few players who other clubs are happy to sell are going to turn your season around? Of course they are.

In the Premier League bad transfer decisions don't just cost a lot of money; they have greater impact than they should because a manager will insist on putting a struggling player into the team if he has spent a fortune on acquiring him. Of course Torres is going to get better. He needs games. He needs to learn our way of playing. He needs to remember what a great footballer he can be.

Meanwhile ... the ship is sinking ... Mayday! Mayday!

Thaler concluded, 'The more we learn about how professional teams work, the more we understand how difficult it is to get everyone in the organisation to adopt strategies that maximise profits and games won. Especially if those strategies violate conventional wisdom.'

Believe me, conventional wisdom is the fuel that runs most of the Premier League.

Smart but unconventional choices may have a mathematically better chance of succeeding, but conventional wisdom is what you follow when you don't want to get fired and you don't want to get beaten. And that's the psychological maxim that limits so many managers and their teams. Getting fired, the fear of losing, these things outweigh the love of winning in almost every case.

We don't get beat, I don't get fired. I don't try anything new, we don't get beat too often, I keep my job. That's success. Here's a theory I have. What is success for a manager measured in these days? Well, if you're asking me, I'd say that it was three years in the same job, when the average is less than 12 months. And nobody looks at what that manager has won. They see, 'Three years? In one job? Hmm ... must be doing something right.'

The trick of management is persuading everybody above and below you that you are a successful high-roller while conservatively playing the percentages. You have to control minds. Then worry about outcomes later.

Managers, like most things in football, go in and out of fashion. That is to say, certain aspects of management become more important on a cyclical basis. Coaching is currently back in vogue. Someday soon we might see a manager on the sideline in a tracksuit and not an Armani. It will remind us of the old days of Shanks, Cloughie and co.

It wasn't always this way. It's true that many years ago managers would have to do everything, from finding the players to coaching them and implementing tactics and laying out and gathering the cones for sessions. (Nobody knows what football did before cones were invented.) But then British football began bastardising the continental model of recruiting specific people to do specific technical jobs. For a while it was messy and uncertain, and some managers wondered if they had any purpose in life apart from wearing a nice suit on Saturday.

During my career, there were many stories of managers who only ever turned up to the training ground on a Friday afternoon, when they would announce the team before heading back home ahead of the match the next day. I can remember being told that Harry Redknapp and Roy Keane preferred that set-up. But coaching is now back in style. Managers are ever more hands-on with their players and mostly they are comfortable with that. Because they carry the can for failure, they are generally control freaks anyway. Delegation might make sense but it doesn't come easy.

There are two great benefits to hands-on coaching: you impart what you know; and you get to know the minds of your players. The better you know your players, the more you can impart and the better you can inspire. Jürgen Klopp's appointment at Liverpool has shown us something that is rarely taken into account by fans because they can't predict it. Managers who have excellent coaching abilities can improve the players who are already in the building, rather than simply buying in new ones.

Brendan Rodgers is a natural hands-on coach too, but rather surprisingly he suffered from a failure to integrate his signings at Liverpool and hence couldn't improve the squad under his vision. Not past a certain point anyway. As a result, the team became disheartened and took their foot off the gas when they saw the vultures darkening the sky over Rodgers' head. When that happens the team begins to lose and the fans get on their backs, and loss of confidence spreads like a virus through the players and the club. That seals the manager's fate as surely as pneumonia kills off many people who went into hospital with other problems.

In the months preceding Rodgers' slow death, I could have found you thousands of comments from Liverpool fans all over the internet claiming that this player should never have been signed and that player should be sold because he wasn't up to it. One of those players was Dejan Lovren, the centre-half bought from Southampton in July 2014 for

£20m, and whose struggle to look anything like a centre-back at Anfield was a little poignant. And another was goalkeeper Simon Mignolet, signed for £10m in the summer of 2013, who struggled badly to find any kind of form. The consensus was that neither of them 'belonged at Anfield'.

After Klopp's arrival in 2015, both players were miraculously transformed and they played pivotal roles in Liverpool reaching the Europa League final last season. Although they would eventually lose 3–1 to Sevilla in the final, both players starred in the competition. They helped Liverpool to beat Manchester United in the last 16 – always a good move if you are a Liverpool player trying to rehabilitate yourself with the faithful.

In the quarter-finals, Lovren scored the winning goal against the favourites for the tournament, Borussia Dortmund, despite Liverpool having, at one point, needed three goals to win the tie. Urban myth (or local news rags) reported that after that game a couple named their newborn baby Lovren. A year or so previously, a Merseyside kid called Lovren would have been condemned to a lifetime of social isolation and mockery.

Such a turnaround can only come about with good coaching, because it involves trust. Trust is one of the most fundamental elements in the transformation of a footballer's fortunes: from trust comes confidence, and then you are in business. For a manager to achieve the trust of his players and have it reciprocated, he must get into the players' heads and find out what makes them want to be the best they can possibly be. Or what it was that made them settle for less under a previous manager. Last season, Jürgen Klopp did that with Liverpool and very nearly landed a trophy within months of arriving at a club that seemed to have lost its way.

Whether you like Klopp or not, and I do, it was good to see a man who specialises in coaching and getting into his players' heads being rewarded by performance on the field. It confirmed everything we always thought we knew about the psychological relationship between players and managers.

José Mourinho was faced with a psychological challenge on his return to Chelsea. At the beginning of last season, when he was under as much pressure as he has ever been, he unwittingly offered us an insight into his man-management skills and the dressing-room tactics designed to get the best out of the hundreds of players he has led into battle during his career.

Interestingly, the former Chelsea manager said in an interview that in his first season back at Chelsea the squad had benefited from 'confrontational leadership'. Mourinho has described this as being 'when you are ready to provoke your players, to try to create some conflict, with the intention to bring out the best from them'. The theory is that friction creates heat and heat creates energy. It works.

Within the game there had long been rumours that key players within the dressing room controlled the squad and, in doing so, controlled the fates of successive managers. Mourinho's second coming at Chelsea had been howled for by so many that he had an advantage going into that dressing room that few other managers would have enjoyed. But he knew the power of the ruling clique. He wondered whether the bigger egos in his dressing room would be able to handle a direct and abrupt approach to their performances on the pitch and their efforts in training. It was a risk, but he had to take it. In the years that he had been away, the players had got used to their own power.

In the end, events proved that he was right to be suspicious. Although Chelsea won the League Cup and the Premier League title in Mourinho's second season back at Stamford Bridge, the following season the players were quick to turn mutinous when Mourinho made a fatal misjudgement: his famed confrontation with his medical staff on the pitch during a 2–2 draw with Swansea.

Incidents like this happen regularly in football, but for Mourinho the timing was wrong and the personalities were wrong. He had spent his first year showing his muscle and effectively saying to the boys, 'You're either with me or against me, and if I have to make an example out of any of you, I will.' Whether he truly believed in that philosophy or not. But he went with it because he knew that at that moment it would work. When he appeared to be bullying medical staff upon whom the players depended, he showed his weakness. He sparked a rebellion against the same confrontational style of management that had served the squad so well the previous year.

You don't have a go at medical staff like that. As players, we forge such close relationships with the medics because some of us spend a lot of time with them. And we find out about their families and their hobbies, and perhaps we'll even become friends and get invited to barbecues and parties, not because we vaguely know each other through work but because we have become friends. The medical staff are out of bounds. Mourinho picked an awful fight. And the players ensured that he lost it. Towards the end, I was even told of a midfielder at Chelsea who had an ankle injury and when the medical department asked him if he could play at the weekend he replied, 'Yes, no problem, but I'm not going to.' Losing the dressing room? That's it. In a soundbite.

Mourinho was eating his Christmas dinner with the players and staff when his phone rang and he walked out, never to be seen again. Sacked.

The lesson: As a manager you must always keep moving and evolving. Last season's tactics might not work this year. The most intriguing thing is that Mourinho didn't even see it coming. He's normally as nimble and alert as a mountain goat. The mutiny at Chelsea will have hurt him and crushed a small part of what many considered an untouchable ego. But ego manifests itself in interesting ways and, in the case of the Special One, I'm sure he will have a burning desire to inflict maximum damage on Chelsea now that he has nailed the Manchester United job.

We say in football that there are two types of player: the ones who need a hug and the ones who need a bollocking. In management there are also two breeds: those who cry when they lose and those who are already planning the next war even before the smoke from the battle has cleared.

When Mourinho hits upon a winning formula, there is no better manager in the game at getting the plan across to his players to execute on the pitch. He achieves his aims through psychological means. He is not the type of manager to become physical with a player, nor is he a shouter. Players I know tell me that his dressing-room presence before matches and at half-time is quiet and downbeat, and generally oriented towards instruction rather than table-pounding.

In a fascinating insight into his man management, Mourinho revealed one of the tactics he employs to coax the best from a player on the pitch: 'I'm not a big guy,' he said, 'how might I do it? Criticise a player in the media – try to provoke a reaction from him of anger, of not being happy with his manager, of trying to show that I am not right.'

But his most intriguing insight came when he recalled a more subtle strategy he'd used to get the best out of Zlatan Ibrahimović when he managed the Swede at Inter Milan during the 2008–9 season. Zlatan has a famously big ego and, like many footballers of that type, he thrives on praise. Whenever Ibrahimović scored, Mourinho would show absolutely no emotion on the bench. He withheld all approval. As a result, Zlatan became increasingly obsessed with performing some deed that would cause Mourinho to react. He scored goals. And then he scored more and more goals.

'Was I aware that it annoyed him? Annoyed, no. But provoke, yes,' Mourinho said.

Zlatan saw the big picture in time. What does it tell you when, presented with the chance to be reunited with Mourinho at Manchester United, Ibrahimović jumped at it? Players always like a manager who a) picks them, and b) makes them better.

The best managerial psychology is always the simplest. Know your subject. Act accordingly.

Ask yourself a question, though. Would you have thought of that? Would you have wound up the mercurial Zlatan in order to improve him? When the whole of the footballing fraternity prefers to stick their tongue down the back of Zlatan's trousers, with entire Instagram accounts devoted to various pearls of wisdom from the Swede, would you have taken the risk that your hunch was right and that your star player would respond as designed? None of you would have, but Mourinho did. That's what makes him the truly great one.

Ask yourself a couple more questions:

If you had decided that deflating Zlatan was the best medicine, how would you have gone about it? Abused him in front of players and staff? Mick McCarthy tried that with Roy Keane in 2002. Ireland played the World Cup without Keane. Would you have dropped him for a bit and risked an epic sulk and a transfer demand? Football history is littered with mistakes like that.

But standing stony-faced when Zlatan scores! How disciplined and subtle is that? Could Zlatan complain to anybody without looking foolish? 'The manager doesn't jump up and down when I score!' And yet Mourinho's passivity gnawed away at Zlatan. I love it. And what I really love about it is the thought process behind it. The deconstruction of an entire personality that the rest of us think we know.

The best managers don't know peace. They torture themselves, agonising over how to improve on what they've just witnessed. How can they make the team play better next time, even if they've won that afternoon? They have a squad of 35 professionals and a large staff and they have to know each one of them intimately in order to extract their best efforts. They have to remember that what is good for one player or staff member isn't necessarily good for all of them, despite the fact that they will all say that everybody should be treated equally.

Mourinho's genius lies in being able to handle so many beasts of different stripes. In 2013–14, the first year of his second coming at Chelsea, he was openly critical of Eden Hazard, who was underperforming. Identifying the reason for his lack of form was crucial.

Same rule for superstars as journeymen.

Is there a problem within the team? No.
Is he underpaid? No.
Has his head been turned by a bigger club? No.
Everything OK in the rest of his life? Yes.
Hiding an injury? No.

OK. So the problem may be a tactical one. Mourinho analysed the games in which he felt Hazard was below par. He went through them like a forensics expert at a crime scene. He saw that Hazard was waiting for the ball to come to him instead of going to get it. Hazard at his best is all about controlling matches in the final third of the pitch with his movement, pace, skill and guile. All of those things had gone. Why?

Mourinho knew the answer. But having the answer was not enough. You can know the answer to everything, but if you can't get it into a player's head in a positive way you may as well not have bothered revising for the test. It's the difference between knowing and doing. Mourinho knew that Hazard wasn't working for the team. He was doing half the job of an elite footballer. For a Mourinho team, it is 'team first, individual second'. Hazard was going to have to shape up or ship out.

The Ibrahimović trick wasn't going to work in this case. For a start, Hazard wasn't scoring any goals and, secondly, he was a very different psychological beast. Hazard didn't advertise his own greatness from the rooftops and billboards. He was diffident and sensitive. He didn't like to discuss his ability and preferred to pass under the radar off the pitch. When his football began to suffer, his sports confidence seeped away. He was committing the cardinal sin. He was hiding.

Mourinho saw it all. He spoke to the press and with one line he solved the Hazard Problem.

'Hazard,' he said, 'is not ready to sacrifice himself 100 per cent for the team.'

Simple. Over to you, Eden.

Hazard now had to show (and quickly) how good he was. Like it or not, he was now under the spotlight in a way that he hadn't been before. It was pressure, but it was a pressure that elite players thrive on. All of those extra cameras and journalists and fans and pundits focused on him, and that stirred something in Hazard. It excited him again.

Hazard's performances picked up. He worked harder for the team and he began scoring again. He looked like an elite footballer once more. The following season Hazard was sensational. He scored 19 goals on his way to winning the PFA Player of the Year as well as Chelsea's Player of the Year. His team romped to the Premier League title, led by their talismanic playmaker. When Hazard scored the winning goal against Manchester United in April, Mourinho declared him to be 'one of the top three players in the world'.

That is top management. It was a pity that Mourinho destroyed it all by using the same techniques on his medical staff. It was a rare and costly miscalculation.

THE SECRET PSYCHOLOGIST INTERRUPTS

A Premier League manager once said to me, 'How do you manage a team of millionaires?' And if you think about it, it's a really good question.

The really interesting word here is 'manage'. You see, the problem with management is that, whether it's in business or football, it's all about control. And it's difficult to use control to drive performance.

The difference between commitment and compliance is significant when it comes to maximising human potential. I think that managers get it wrong when they take the title too literally. Gary Megson, for example, was constantly fretting over what the big names in the dressing room were saying about him, so he tried to tighten the reins further. So much so that at one stage he employed a henchman, Chris Evans, to do his iron-fisted bidding. But possessive control and paranoia are almost always guaranteed to bring about the end of any relationship.

The example of Mourinho's management style is much more about leadership than control. Perhaps if managers viewed themselves as leaders, if they discerned more clearly that their role was to sell vision, to devise strategies to optimise individual talent and inspire and motivate performance, then we might see a difference in the way they apply their talent.

In my Introduction, I mentioned that talent is not enough. This is as true for a manager as it is for a player. All the footballing knowledge in the world is worthless unless it can be imparted in a way that secures engagement and traction. When I work with managers, I use a four-step process that gets the players onside psychologically, rather than imposing the manager's will: imagination – illustration – participation – integration. Gary Speed used this method when he took over as Wales manager. The fruits of this technique are in evidence in Chris Coleman's side today.

1. Imagination is where you sell a vision of what you are trying to achieve. The selling bit is essential. Capturing people's imagination with regard to 'what might be' is the key to obtaining an emotional commitment. Selling is an important part of leadership.

2. Illustration is the part where you show people how you're going to do it. This is all about strategy and tactics. This is where you demonstrate that there is a method and approach geared towards achieving the goals you've stated.

3. Participation is about allowing people to contribute. This is not necessarily about being democratic; more about consultation and co-authorship. There are some talented players in a squad and some experienced backroom staff. Encouraging people to participate in the plan and tactics is a great way to get a buy-in. Having alignment is key to gaining support and understanding.

I have worked with three Premier League football teams, all of which were in the bottom three at Christmas. The first thing we did was break the remaining games into chunks of three. We then grouped the players by unit (defenders, midfield, attacking players etc.) and asked what could be expected in terms of points in the next three games. We then asked each group, very simply, what their contribution would be. So, for example, the defenders were asked, 'How many goals will you score in the next three games? How many clean sheets will we have?'

Interestingly, when the defenders were asked about the goals, they began to imagine and consider what was possible. It might be just one goal, but they still started to discuss where, when and who that goal might come from ... and so goals from our defenders appeared. Simply by debating possibilities, a target such as 'one goal in the next three' for the defensive players became front of mind. Importantly, this was not an imposed objective, but something that was discussed and decided upon by the players.

4. *Integration* is about making it a reality. Ensuring that your way of doing things is embedded. This is as much a cultural shift as it is an operational one; establishing a way of doing things that is directly reflective of the type of environment you wish to create. One of the most difficult things to do as a manager is manage the mood at a club. For all his recently exposed faults, Sam Allardyce is the best manager I have known when it comes to maintaining a constant and consistent atmosphere. Whatever you think of Sam's tactics, he really is a superb manager in terms of working with people and teams. Big Sam's ability to take an approach that drives consistency of thinking is one of his greatest assets. I believe that consistency of mind leads to consistency of play, and the more a manager can keep a constant mood in the camp, the better. The right level of stress enables performance; the wrong level is distress, which inhibits performance through interfering with thinking.

There is a 'triangle of performance' which I have used with a variety of teams. To ensure optimum performance you should have all three. I know we're talking about management in football, but please also consider this in the context of the workplace.

Want
Why What

People have to know what to do; they have to know why they're doing it; and they have to want to do it. Tick these three off – well done, you've got high performance. However, as a manager, you'll often see people with just two of these criteria. For example, you may have someone who knows what to do and why they should do it ... you know what, though, they just can't be arsed – they don't want to do it. On the other hand, you may have someone who really wants to do something and knows why they've got to do it, but they simply don't know how to – they are missing the 'what' element.

Although all three are important, whenever people tell me that they can't get their team to do something, I always ask, 'Is the "why" big enough?' You see, the 'why' bit is the most important. If you can create a big enough 'why', people don't even need to know the how. In extreme circumstances, when the 'why' is important enough, people just find a way. You'd be amazed how many of your friends and family could climb a tree for the first time if they were being chased by a lion.

As a manager, it's important to cover these three areas with your team as a whole, but also to spend time understanding and creating the individual 'why'. This may seem time costly, but tailors have an adage: 'measure twice, cut once'. Put the effort in early to understand the player's individual motivations and hot buttons, and it saves you having to do it later, perhaps under more difficult circumstances.

7. FEAR

Risk and how to tackle it

Goalkeepers are mad. Unless you are Kasper Schmeichel and the madness is in the blood, who would want to be a keeper? They were the gangly kids who came down for football, got stuck in goal and were left there no matter how much they whined to be let out for just 10 minutes. You know, those long strings of awkwardness who had an optimism that couldn't be dented? They quit or they became goalies.

They were separated from the herd early. Taken away to do their own training. Taught not to flinch even if a bullet is coming their way. Made as flexible as gymnasts, as resilient as honey badgers and as mad as hatters. The coach told them they were great at goalkeeping, just to keep them happy. Anybody could let five in. No shame in being nutmegged. Even twice.

So they learned to stand in front of hostile crowds, often their own hostile crowds, listening to abuse for 90 minutes. Most of the invective came from behind them. Sometimes it came from the 10 teammates in front of them. Their only relief was to punctuate the torment with the odd save. The crowd would ooh and aah and applaud. That needed to happen on average about 10 times a game for the crowd to learn to trust the keeper. And if it was 10 times a game, then chances are that another two were getting past him and he would be shunted off.

They grow at a different rate from the rest of us. They get into the team later but they last longer. In Italy last season, AC Milan gave a debut to Gianluigi Donnarumma. Milan had signed him as a 14-year-old in 2013 for 250,000 euros. When he was 15, he sat on the Milan bench in Serie A. At 16, he made his debut and played 30 games last season. The youngest keeper to start a match in the history of Italian football.

He is exceptional. I can't remember a teenage goalkeeper ever breaking through to a Premier League team, let alone a 16-year-old. Most keepers have a long gestation period. Kasper Schmeichel won his first Premiership medal at the same age his father did, 29. He had been at Manchester City, Darlington, Bury, Falkirk, Cardiff City, Coventry City, Notts County and Leeds United as he learned his trade (you can't say that the family surname helped him cut any corners). For an outfield player, the end of your playing days is in sight at 29. For a keeper there can be 10 years left.

John Burridge, for instance, played at 29 professional clubs, and made his Premier League debut for Manchester City at the age of 43. He began playing in 1969, when the Beatles were still together, and didn't finish until 1997, two years after the Oasis–Blur war had peaked. So the goalies are the old men of the dressing room, still throwing themselves about on muddy fields when they ought to know better. They are the only players on the field whose mistakes get punished 99 times out of 100. Madness makes them what they are.

The history of their madness can be charted back to the early days. In one of the earliest penalties in an FA Cup final, awarded in 1922 to Huddersfield Town, as the kicker placed the ball, James Mitchell, the Preston keeper, began running, skipping and jumping back and forth along his goal line, howling like a banshee and waving his arms as if to attract an aeroplane to land and rescue him.

Huddersfield scored anyway and a disapproving FA had a festival of tut-tutting about ungentlemanly conduct before changing the rules about goalkeepers' conduct.

There are a lot of rules of management, but in the top three of any textbook would be the need to remember one thing: Goalkeepers are mad. Handling goalkeepers is a key test of a manager's skills.

As a group, goalkeepers mostly train separately from the rest of us, happily performing all sorts of physical contortions before trotting back to us, pathetically begging for somebody to take shots at them. Within the main group they are generally quiet. On the field, where there is increasing emphasis on the business of game management, they are loud and hectoring. Then they go off and room together and bitch about the rest of us.

Still, they fascinate because the psychological pressures on them are different from those on the other members of the team. The penalty for failure is substantially higher.

I spent a lot of time watching Paul Robinson. Not stalking him, but for me as a Spurs fan, his time with the club always promised more than it delivered. He was a meticulous keeper who never gave a hint of eccentricity in his pomp. His relentless positive thinking and bravery made him the success he had dreamed of being. 'Success thinking', as the Secret Psychologist calls it. The sadness is what happened to

TSF PSYCHOLOGICAL TIPS: GOALKEEPERS THINK DIFFERENTLY

Paul Robinson, the former Leeds, Spurs and Blackburn goalkeeper, became an international not just because of his talent but more importantly because he was able to apply his talent with success thinking. When the ball is hit high and long, many goalkeepers will think, 'Should I go for this?' Then they have to decide quickly whether the answer is yes or no. Paul used to think differently. When the ball was hit high and long into his area, his first reaction was, 'I must go for this.' His default setting was that he must claim this ball. After making the decision and physically committing, he would then ask whether he needed to.

Paul Robinson, in an England jersey in October 2006, when he was at his peak.

England were playing Croatia in Zagreb. Robinson was one game away from equalling Gordon Banks' record of seven clean sheets on the trot. People were beginning to speak about Paul Robinson in the same sentence as some of the all-time great English goalkeepers: Banks, Clemence, Shilton etc.

For the first hour against Croatia he was perfection. England were experimenting with three centre-halves and it just wasn't working. The exposure tested Robinson and only a series of world-class saves kept the Croats scoreless. Then it all unravelled. In the 61st minute, Niko Kovač floated a hopeful cross. Robinson, always reliable in the air, came forward but wrong-footed himself and Da Silva looped an easy header over him and into the net.

Bad.

And worse was to follow. Eight minutes later, Gary Neville knocked a routine back pass in Robinson's direction. It was hit soft and from Robinson's right. The keeper came out, with the intention of launching the ball deep downfield. Just as he was about to connect, the ball twitched like some novelty toy, bobbled over his foot and rolled into the England net.

Robinson was never quite the same again. He kept his place until the qualifiers were over, but the following August, when England played their first international at the new Wembley, he made another howler to give Germany their first goal in a 2–1 win. He was taken off at half-time.

The nerves seemed shot through by then. In a later match, against Russia, he palmed a shot into the path of Roman Pavlyuchenko, who went on to score the winner. And believe me, as a Spurs fan, conceding to Roman Pavlyuchenko is no mean feat.

Robinson never started for England again.

Things had also gone downhill at White Hart Lane and in the summer of 2008 he left for Blackburn Rovers. The abiding memory from his final season was a nightmare FA Cup game against Reading. The game ended in a two-all draw but Reading's goals were a comedy of goal-keeping errors.

What was shocking about that period of Robinson's career was watching him struggle with the things he had always been good at. He was once a goalkeeper who came to high balls with confidence and authority. By the time of the Reading FA Cup game, his nerves were such that he caught a harmless 45-yard free-kick with nobody near him, but then managed to jump back over his own line to concede a goal. A sure sign of a player thinking too much about something that was once routine.

I once played with a goalkeeper whose default setting was the polar opposite to Paul Robinson's approach when he was at his peak. My teammate decided that whenever the ball was crossed, it was basically nothing to do with him. He never came off his line for the simple reason that he had no confidence in the outcome. He didn't believe that he was a safe pair of hands when his feet weren't on the ground.

If he absolutely had to intervene, then he would punch the ball. In these situations, he was still rooted to his goal line and was always reluctant to leave the ground – fearing in his madness, perhaps, that he wouldn't come back down again. So he didn't jump and had no momentum behind his punched clearances, and often the ball just looped in the air and dropped down near the penalty spot.

Though he was a tremendous shot-stopper, making saves is only a very small part of being a goalkeeper. He certainly wasn't the person to blame for the club's relegation that year, but there were games that we could have won but lost because of his inhibitions about crosses.

The problem with both keepers should have been easy to recognise. If we were dealing with behavioural economics instead of mad goalies, we would note straight away that humans are risk averse (when we face uncertainty we attempt to reduce that uncertainty) and loss averse (we weigh losses as being greater than gains). So, certifiable as goalies may be, it makes sense in their brains not to come off the line when their confidence is low: the gain involved in making a routine catch is heavily outweighed by the loss of screwing up.

Most of the time, when a goal goes in, the goalkeeper recovers his confidence and composure with a bit of positive denial. That is, he bawls at and abuses his 10 colleagues who let the ball get past them before he did the same. The reaction is immediate and they must teach it at goalkeeping school. Ball goes in. Keeper starts hurling insults at anybody within earshot. Alex Stepney, the old Manchester United goalie, once had to be hospitalised after dislocating his jaw from shouting too hard. Honest.

But the dropped cross, the flapping in the air, the catastrophic second-guessing, these things are so public and humiliating that no amount of hollering and carry-on will convince the audience or the manager that it was anybody else's fault. If the goalkeeper comes for the ball, the goalkeeper must get the ball. Simple as that. There is no middle ground.

Maybe keepers are wired differently, but when it comes to loss and risk they are the same as the rest of us. One loss or failed risk impacts the way we feel about future events. A goalkeeper who has royally screwed up once or twice will weigh future scenarios in the light of those failures. If he doesn't, somebody else will remind him. Many years ago, the blunder-prone Leeds United goalie, Gary Sprake, inadvertently threw the ball into his own net at Liverpool. I don't know why, he just did. There was a minute plus injury time before half-time. As the players trooped off to the dressing rooms, the Anfield PA rang out with the song 'Careless Hands'.

With my teammate, who had a worse phobia about crosses than Jesus had, and with Paul Robinson, who generally got crucified, maybe the solution was to take them out of the firing line for a while. Not as punishment but for rehab. Let them build the confidence back up with a bit of positive coaching.

Look at other players on the field. Very few of them have been cured of the same disease.

For a footballer, fucking up under pressure is that dream you have of going to work and realising that you're sat at your desk naked and fat. Everybody is looking at you and pointing. So the default setting for many players is, 'Don't make a mistake.' What they should be saying is, 'This is going to work. It is going to work because I have done it successfully so many times that it can't fail.'

But the fear justifies itself in hindsight. You can spot the players who are scared of making mistakes. They are so scared of making mistakes that they end up making mistakes. As a Spurs fan, I've seen several down the years and I've played against a few too. Michael Dawson was terrible for it when he first went to Spurs, and Kyle Walker is similar now.

Walker is interesting because he has so much pace that his control has never been as good as it should be. He works on the basis that if he runs down the wing to cross the ball, he'll overhit his first touch before the cross because he'll be able to catch the ball anyway. But the pitch is only so big. Watch how many times he gets into the last tenth of the pitch and knocks the ball off for a goal-kick because there isn't enough pitch left to catch up with the ball. It's like watching Forrest Gump. I know it sounds harsh. But just watch him. You'll see it with your own eyes.

In fact, it is symptomatic of fast players that their touch suffers as a result of their pace. Which leads to a dangerous knock-on effect. There are areas of the pitch where a fine touch and good control are compulsory. Those needs cannot be sidestepped, even with pace. I could make a compilation of underhit and overhit back passes that Walker has made to his goalkeeper over the years as a result of his poor touch and feel for the ball. And that has eaten away at his confidence when he is the last man back. As a result, when he is closed down and only has one touch, he gets it wrong. Often.

Also, watch his throw-ins. Walker's default setting – and his manager Mauricio Pochettino is probably not helping here by asking Walker to return the ball into play as quickly as possible – is to throw the ball to Toby Alderweireld, who is always 10 yards behind Walker in his own half. Now, there is nothing wrong with keeping possession, and indeed that is how Spurs play, but what is striking is that Walker doesn't even entertain the possibility of looking forward, ever, even accidentally.

What makes me suspect that this isn't all about Spurs' playing style is that in the left-hand berth Tottenham have two players in Danny Rose and Ben Davies whose first reaction when taking a quick throw is always to look forward. Rose, in particular, with his long throw will look forward, and when Davies picks the ball up after it has gone out of play he turns to face the pitch looking up the line, not back. He may throw it back but he looked forward first. Walker doesn't do that. It does cost Spurs occasionally, when teams are able to resume their shape quickly.

But for all that Walker is a decent enough player. His pace causes coaches to overlook other defects. This is football's version of the halo effect. The halo effect is our tendency to judge somebody in a positive way because of a known positive trait. The most basic demonstration is the difference in the attention we give if somebody attractive stops us to ask for directions as opposed to somebody we find singularly unattractive. We don't know anything more about either of them other than that they are lost but, yes, we are that superficial.

Even in sport we reward attractiveness. Would Beckham be one of the richest men in all the galaxies if he had a face like a pug but the same skills? No. In football, when it comes to the halo effect, coaches and scouts are suckers for pace. Pace makes them go weak at the knees. They'll bleed out or explain away worrying attributes like poor touch or excessive caution.

Look at him, he runs like a gazelle.

But he has the first touch of a gazelle too.

I'm not listening to you. I'm not listening.

(The flipside is the pitchfork or devil effect. If we decide we don't like someone, it is almost impossible for them to redeem themselves. Bad early impressions are amazingly resilient. Just ask Wayne Rooney.)

But back to goalkeepers and loss aversion.

When I started my career I played with a giant of a goalkeeper, somebody who you could look up to literally and figuratively. He was a guy you could depend on no matter what. As a goalkeeper he was outstanding. He made the best save I have ever seen on a football pitch in an away game against Brentford. Remember the Gordon Banks save? It was like that but the header was faster and lower and it was better because I want it to be. He had the shot-stopping but he had everything else too. And he was one of the least risk-averse men I have seen in the game. He put the tightrope up every day without a net underneath and proceeded to take the piss out of everybody down below.

In training terms, our squad was not the greatest. We were a hotchpotch of kids trying to learn the trade, a few players signed out of non-league and a couple of veterans who had played in League One and League Two for their whole careers. It wasn't the academy of the stars. Scars more like.

Lots of former Premier League players on their way down would have tossed off the last year or two of their careers. Why? Because they have everything to lose. As the skills decline and a player slips down the league, milking the game for a few last paydays, the obvious thing is to explain the new circumstance with a shrug of the shoulders. 'I don't give a fuck. I've been there, done that. Nothing left to prove.' But this goalkeeper, as he got older, he got hungrier and hungrier, and his desire to improve the players around him and drag them up to his level was remarkable. He got into the heads of our strikers like no opposition player I have ever seen. He hounded them like no coach I have ever seen. He made the strikers want to kill him with the ball in training. They wanted to drive football-shaped holes in his chest.

In training, he would save everything that was flung at him when we did shooting practice at the end of the session. But rather than gloat he would make it more personal. He would accuse the players of not caring as much as he did. That's actually worse than just being called a shit player by a teammate. It's like when your dad says to you, 'I'm not angry, I'm just disappointed.'

Something would snap inside the players. They'd get angry. Everybody hated being accused of not caring as much as a teammate, especially as he had been to the big league already and we hadn't. The strikers took it to heart more than most because not only was their commitment being doubted, but they realised that their talent was also being called into question. So they tried harder. They hit the ball harder, they concentrated more, they tried to be more accurate and they focused more intently on the ball as they made their connection.

Putting one past him was a joy. It was vindication. Of course, everybody muttered comments under their breath when they eventually began to score against him. 'Get that out the net then, you foreign cunt.' But it had worked. Ultimately, he had won. Before he called everybody out, nobody had cared as much as he did. It showed every day in everything we did.

I learned so much from that man. I learned that the strength we have inside us, our physical reserves and the levels that people can reach are extraordinary. For most of us, those things only come out when we really, really care, when the very fabric of what we stand for is directly questioned. From that time on, I cared about football every single day. I wanted to be the best player on any pitch I played on.

Our old goalkeeper put himself on the line every day with us. He could have called us out and then not delivered a single save as we rained shots on him. And we would have laughed at the old fool.

If sport is as much about confidence as we think it is, then confidence, or fear, is contagious. Look at Germany v Brazil in the 2014 World Cup. The 7–1 game. Perfect example. When a team gets bopped and the manager looks shaken and shattered afterwards, it's a good bet that the same will happen the next week and the dressing room will be muttering that the gaffer doesn't know what he is doing anymore. Bad days are never about shouting, I realise that now. They are about putting confidence back as quickly as possible.

Much of the confidence I had in my career I caught from that great goalkeeper. Guys with as much talent were too afraid of risk or loss to put it on the line every day, to just say, 'Give me the fucking ball because I really know what I am doing.' Put yourself under that pressure and deliver and people will follow you to the gates of hell. Or the New Den. Same thing.

I might call that old foreign goalkeeper now if I can find his number. Not surprisingly, he went on to become a very solid coach. A bit of goalkeepers' madness and a ton of confidence proved to be the perfect mix.

I've nothing to lose and everything to learn.

THE SECRET PSYCHOLOGIST INTERRUPTS

I once heard somebody say that confidence is like a muscle – the more you exercise it, the bigger it gets. And this is sort of true. Do the thing you fear, and watch the fear diminish. Apparently, the number-one fear in this country is public speaking ... followed by death. If this is true, it means that most people would rather be in the casket than giving the eulogy!

Players will often ask me, 'How can I reduce fear?' or 'How can I increase my confidence?' The two questions share a similar root cause.

Most fears are based around the dread of failure. Some players can get into a mindset of not wanting to be the one

THE SECRET PSYCHOLOGIST: SOME OF THE PLAYERS WHO YOU THINK WEAR THEIR HEART ON THEIR SLEEVES ARE REALLY JUST SCARED LITTLE BOYS

El Hadji Diouf wasn't everyone's cup of tea, but no one can deny that at times he could be one of the most sensational players in the Premier League. A precocious talent, one day in conversation he gave a profound insight into his approach to football.

He said: 'You must always ask yourself a question: Do you play to get the cheers or do you play to avoid the boos?' In other words, do you set out not to make a mistake (avoid the boos) or do you play to be the match winner (get the cheers)? Whatever you think of Diouf, he committed to a personal brand, something that he stood for, and understood his purpose in the game.

who loses the game, and are motivated by this more so than wanting to be the one who wins it. The paradox is that the more you try not to make mistakes, the more likely you are to do so. We are drawn towards our most dominant thought. Expectation becomes reality, and we do get what we think about, even if it is something we don't want to happen. A penalty-taker repeating the mantra 'Don't hit it over the bar' or 'Don't scuff this' is the same as a golfer standing on the first tee and thinking, 'Don't hit it left' or 'Don't drop it in the water.'

It's the old one about trying not to think about a dog or a white bear. We have to construct a thought to deconstruct it. We have to think about it in order not to think about it. So if you are thinking about not wanting something to happen, you are actually just indulging in negative goal-setting.

The best way for a player not to make mistakes and to move away from the fear of doing so is to be motivated by what they wish to achieve, not by what they wish to avoid. By being expansive in their thinking and ambitions to win, they are more likely to give themselves the best opportunity of playing well by expressing their natural talent. It is also important for us as human beings to remember that we will make mistakes – it doesn't make *us* a mistake. We can fail – it doesn't make *us* a failure. We must detach the action from the person. If we don't, it becomes personal and internalised in a way that erodes confidence.

Also, mistakes are often not as costly as our reaction to them. Let me explain. Often, the person who wins a big golf tournament, like the Masters or the Open, is not the one who makes the fewest mistakes – it's the person who responds to the mistakes he makes the best. It's about comeback. Comeback leads to resilience, and resilience breeds confidence. You could almost argue that the more failures we have, the greater the opportunity to build confidence.

I think this mindset is potentially more important for defenders than attacking players. Attacking players miss a scoring opportunity, and in the context of the game it is soon forgotten. A defender makes a mistake, a goal is conceded and the focus switches to the player. Defenders can make many great tackles and blocks over the period of a game or even a season, but it seems always to be the mistakes that are remembered. It underlines for me the fact that we must detach the act from the person.

If a player makes a mistake, his and the team's confidence can be affected; the mistake may then be compounded. But if a mistake is made and the player responds well to the incident, he and the team may indeed play better as a result.

I remember Benítez often told his players before they went out to 'enjoy being on the ball', and in my view it's really good advice. I think the big players relish the big occasion. It is seen as an opportunity to showcase their talent. They know that nothing can be achieved without passion and energy, and more importantly realise that their talent will be stifled by nerves and tension.

We often see professionals revert to being amateurs when it comes to performing under pressure. The best example being the dreaded heartbreaking, nail-biting penalty shoot-out. It is at this point – when our critical mind, the one we use for 'thinking' not just 'doing', gets involved – that we become compromised. The more confident we feel, the more we can rely on the 'just doing'.

The best players on the world stage know that their talent is innate. It is part of them and they can rely on it. They vividly imagine scoring the winning or opening goal, and making the essential tackles. They tap into their rich personal history and evidence of performing, which is stored in their minds from previous world-stage encounters.

You can do the same. If you keep a 'three of the best' diary, you can use it to recall your magic moments. The evening after each game you play, just write down the three best things you did today. No matter how shit your game was (even if you were sent off in the first minute), take this seriously and write down three things that you did great. It might be an important tackle or block; it might just be a jinking run or a decent throw-in. Things that aren't quantifiable are fine too. Perhaps you put in a bit of effort when normally you wouldn't have bothered. Or maybe you accepted a decision when usually you would have kicked off. If you keep reminding yourself of the three worthwhile things you did every game, you'll be surprised how, over time, it fuels your confidence.

The other important aspect of confidence is that it is dynamic. It's changeable for some players depending upon certain factors. It's amazing how some players are more confident in certain competitions or against certain opposition. The best players will not be overawed by the significance of a game or whether they are 'worthy' to be in it. They will revel in the personal and team glory afforded to them by doing what they do best. By not thinking about technique or being distracted by practical thoughts, they are free to express themselves through their natural skills and expertise.

The pitch, the ball, your boots do not care whether it's a pre-season warm-up or the FA Cup final. It is only thoughts about the importance of a game or achieving certain outcomes that can result in some individuals losing confidence. Take away the meaning, and see the opportunity to express yourself and be true to your skills by keeping your thinking consistent.

8. PURPOSE

Finding it – and holding on to it

In his hugely influential book, *Thinking, Fast and Slow*, Daniel Kahneman quotes a study of golfers to demonstrate the impact of something called prospect theory.

Two economists at the University of Pennsylvania analysed 2.5 million putts by golfers. Now, I am still sexually active so I don't play golf, but I do understand why the economists put themselves through this torture. Golf is unique in that it explicitly states what level of performance is adequate. The idea of par is a perfect reference point for economists. Par is the baseline for a good but not outstanding performance. No golfer celebrates scoring a par unless he has somehow escaped the jaws of some greater disaster.

The two economists, Devin Pope and Maurice Schweitzer, compared two situations in which a player might find himself when close to the hole:

- Putting to avoid a bogey
- Putting to achieve a birdie

In theory, in golf every stroke should count equally. A shot is a shot, after all. You hit the ball and it adds to your score for the round. But, in prospect theory, some strokes count more than others: failing to make par from a putt represents a loss; making a birdie is a gain.

So, God love them, the men studied the 2.5 million putts in excruciating detail and they discovered that what they had expected to be true was, in fact, true. No matter how hard or easy the putt was, the golfers were 3.6 per cent more successful when putting to save par than they were when putting to make a birdie.

That doesn't sound like much, but consider Tiger Woods, one of the subjects in the study. If, in his best years, Tiger had putted for birdies as successfully as he did to save par, he would have reduced his per-tournament score by a shot each week. That would have represented a gain of a million dollars a year.

Translated into football terms, we can assume (correctly) that Tiger Woods in his pomp was the Germany or Spain of golf. He expected to win, as opposed to avoid loss. Who would represent England in this analogy? I don't know enough about golf to be familiar with the names of players that far down the rankings.

I know this, though. Even though they always say the right things before tournaments and we almost always believe them, the English players' fear of loss is far greater than their appetite to win. They are more desperate to save par than they are to score a birdie.

Defeat for the England football team involves the whole trauma that we have become familiar with over the years. Disillusionment. Blame. Tabloid abuse. Hindsight analysis that turns every well-meant step into a catastrophe. Players become pariahs and laughing stocks. Managers get sacked. Is it any wonder they want to save footballing par much more desperately than they want to score a birdie?

The problem is that in football the playing-for-par mentality is directly interfered with by the awkward presence of other teams who see playing England as the opportunity to score a handy birdie. So England get turned over as a result of their own fears: the greater the prospect of defeat, the worse we get. Give us a 2–0 head start and we can look good enough to beat anybody. Put us 2–1 down to Iceland and England look like a pub team playing together for the first time.

So, at Euro 2016, when Germany played the hosts, France, it represented the 20th time out of 26 major tournament appearances that the Germans have reached a semi-final. They lost, went home and made quiet, thoughtful adjustments to their game, after a thorough review process. England's team, which has only once in its history reached a tournament semi-final outside of English soil, came home and tearfully stuck their heads into the stocks down at the village green so we could all chuck rotten fruit and veg at them.

We saw them as the reason for our football failure, not as a symptom of it. Pretty soon we would be back to the business of believing that the Premier League is the greatest football league on the planet and a further example of what we have so generously given to the world in terms of football.

Mainly what we have given is a lot of laughs.

Our perception of England's failures and our shallow, repetitive analysis of each fresh disaster seem to me to represent two easily identifiable psychological conditions.

FIRST: NEGATIVITY BIAS

In negativity bias, the bad things have a more powerful effect on us than the good – as we saw in the previous chapter with loss aversion. We weigh errors and screw-ups as being heavier and more significant than successes and what we do right. In other words, something very positive will generally have less of an impact on a person's behaviour and cognition than something equally impactful but negative.

I read a blog recently which spoke about wide receivers in the NFL. The writer pointed out that fans and analysts are obsessed with the number of times a wide receiver drops a pass from the quarterback. Successful completions don't register quite so much.

For example, Amari Cooper of the Oakland Raiders dropped the ball 18 times in 2015. This was just about all that people knew about Amari Cooper. But the Raiders attempted 606 passes in the course of the season and Cooper ran 592 pass routes and played 85 per cent of the snaps. His rate of drops as opposed to successful execution was 3 per cent. Of course, Cooper would like to get his rate of drops down, but the important thing from a coaching point of view is to keep emphasising what he is doing *right*, not to make him afraid to run pass routes and go hiding because the weight of the emotional impact of dropping the ball is far greater than the reward for catching it.

That's what has happened to England players. When disaster looms, they would prefer to hide and not run the routes at all rather than risk dropping the ball. We think that they live in a bubble, isolated by their money from the world around them. Truth is, their reality is constructed by all of us as fans and critics, but experienced privately by players.

It's fun to pile in and give them a kicking, but that's how we help them to fail the next time.

SECOND: WHAT YOU SEE IS ALL THERE IS

The classic illustration Kahneman gives is one in which he shows us a picture of somebody who might be a leader and says the words 'strong and charismatic'. We automatically leap ahead of him and decide that person would be a good leader. In other words, we grasp some obvious elements of a story and our brains fill in the narrative around it. But two words aren't enough to decide on a person's leadership potential. The next word out of Kahneman's mouth might have been 'corrupt', but we don't look for or wait for more information.

What you see is all there is – and at big tournaments what we see is England players failing. Therefore, they have to be to blame. They don't want it enough. They are too rich and pampered. They aren't leaders. They aren't role models. Are they even men?

An obvious example is the treatment of young England players in the days after Iceland beat them at Euro 2016. Hindsight distorts everything, and the squad that were so young and refreshing and quietly fancied when they set off for France were coming home as overpaid, overhyped failures.

It is interesting to note that when the boys departed for France, the country they left behind was still part of the EU. By the time they got home, Brexit had revealed a tectonic fault line through the home nation, and the same forces of spite and envy and rage behind that vote were brought to bear on mere footballers. By losing to Iceland, the team lacked the moral fibre that we like to imagine holds the entire country together. Barney Ronay of the *Guardian* caught the mood well:

> There are three main routes of attack here. The first is outright spiteful muck-raking, the suggestion that defeat is a consequence of complete moral, personal and spiritual collapse. England's players have already been convicted of, in no specific order, greed, yobbery, ornate plumbing, owning a telephone, wearing headphones, going to parties, being soft-skinned nancy boys, having inappropriately attractive girlfriends, and generally revealing themselves to be overgrown men-child monsters ...

In football, the most glaring psychological problem, as far as the media is concerned (and the public, for that matter), is the amount of money that young players are paid. It is a conundrum for many commentators and fans alike, and very often it inspires a raft of other psychological traits in the observer, but mostly it induces jealousy.

When England returned from France, Adam Lallana was torn apart for having a deal with a face-cream company, Joe Hart got a similar going-over, Kyle Walker became a 'hippy crack idiot', Wayne Rooney got the abuse he has grown up with (thick, sadly overweight solicitor of grannies) – and they all got off lightly compared to Raheem Sterling, who experienced the same current of racism that the Brexiteers had been channelling. He wasn't young, gifted and black, and to be cherished for all those reasons. He was a symbol of moral decay; his private life was rummaged through by journalists behaving like starving raccoons behind a diner.

Raheem Sterling is a 22-year-old kid who happens to be very good at football and not great yet at dealing with the pressures that come with it. He's not asking to be prime minister or Archbishop of Canterbury.

Of course, it brings a little smile to our lips when somebody young and cocky gets a timely kick in the ass – it did to mine – but it reminded me too of a time when I was young and cocky. I certainly wouldn't have needed to be held up to the nation as an example of everything that is wrong in life. In sport, cockiness is not always what it seems. It's an armour and a weapon. If you go out strutting and looking confident, then you have a better chance of performing.

Though jealousy is a perfectly natural emotion, it is important to consider, if only to help you battle your green-eyed monster, the incredible amount of work, by hundreds of people, that goes into finding the next £20,000-a-week teenager. And it is also important to appreciate that the wage is so high (often before the player has kicked a professional ball) because of a wide range of market forces pertaining to competition and his ongoing playing and commercial potential.

There is a temptation to blame the player for his success and remuneration, and that is unfortunate at best; at worst, it is the sort of stupid fucking shit that you'd hear two meatheads discussing at a bar in France while they're tear-gassed by the local police for singing songs about ISIS.

And there is another issue to contend with for young players making it in the game at the highest level: the fact that it is hard to get there, but even harder to stay there. So many players are earning a relative fortune while at the top of their games, but within a few years are playing in the lower leagues. There are many psychological reasons for why this might happen, but for me probably the most common are the following three:

1. *A lack of belief.* To play at the highest level you have to believe you are fully capable. In a pressurised environment in full view of others, a crack of doubt becomes a chasm. Professional sport, not just football, has a way of not merely exposing weakness, but actually exacerbating it. Not only is the blade of self-doubt stuck in firmly, it is also twisted.

The dynamic for a player is always changing. A youngster comes in who is treated like a welcome upstart, there to put pressure on the established players and jostle and push for a position in the first team. That young player may then become a consistent talent, a recognised starter in a particular position. However, at some stage the hunter will become the hunted. Someone will be after that spot in the team. The player may not play for a few months due to injury, or have a period of doing not so well, or the dynamic may change due to contract negotiations or something else that changes his own perception of himself.

Lack of belief comes along and pokes a hole where your confidence once stood in all sorts of ways. It might not necessarily be about questioning your talent like the above example, or the player who misses a string of free-kicks and then retreats from future opportunities. There are other ways too. A player once told me that Morten Gamst Pedersen was a top-flight player worthy of turning a few heads at the top four clubs at the time, until he got clattered by Gary Neville. It was suggested that he was never the same player again. The player told me they knew that if there was a 50:50 ball with Pedersen he'd be soft. Players can also struggle to come back from injury with the same level of conviction.

2. *Continued application.* Another reason why young players can't maintain the standard to play at the top level is application. A magician friend said to me that one of the rules of magic is 'practise until it's perfect, and then when it's perfect, practise some more'. It needs to be the same in top-flight football. A player may also fall away quickly in their career

because they think they've made it. Got the contract and got the shirt, and the goal has been achieved.

It's surprising how many players, on reaching their desired level of success, will then change their routine or the actions that enabled them to get to that place. It's funny, but when you think about it, a change in title often brings about a change in the way in which we perceive ourselves. We believe we need to be different now, and move away from what we were. If someone becomes a manager, they then think they have to become managerial, as if needing a different level of maturity or new approach. If you become a father or a mother, you feel that things have to be different now. Labels change us, sometimes for the better and sometimes for the worse.

A taxi driver I spoke to recently said that if he was a Premier League player, he'd be shagging and partying all the time ... No more questions, your honour. Now let me ask you a question: if you had a cashpoint in your living room and once a month you went up to it and pressed a button and 70 grand came out, what would you do to maintain it? How much would you invest in making sure that machine kept doing it?

You see, Premiership football is a contract that many players don't fully appreciate. Football has said to the player, 'I'll give you everything, adulation, recognition, money, fame, travel, all you'll ever want – all you have to do is train, practise, learn and respect your talent.' Not a bad deal really, is it?

3. The search for perfection. If you're serious about your talent and you're a hard worker, you may still be in trouble. In all the sports I have worked in, I can honestly say that players who try to find perfection are vulnerable to chasing the wrong goals. In my experience, if you look for perfection, two things happen. You either get disappointed and frustrated because you never find it, or you find it and then spend all your time worrying about when you're going to lose it.

This is going to sound weird, but players try to be technically too good. As humans, we spend a lot of time thinking about what we haven't got, what we should have done, what we could do better. We spend a lot of time thinking about our weaknesses and trying to fix them. This in itself is a problem. We try to fix our issues and they seem to get worse. I've had people come to me and say, 'I'm a procrastinator, I need to stop procrastinating.' And then they find that the problem gets worse: they have now labelled themselves as a procrastinator, and so that's what they become.

When a young player hits the big leagues, he may also have to contend with what I call the 'paradise complex'. This is where someone gets a lot very quickly. They then self-sabotage. They believe that they are not worthy of it and shouldn't be there. They believe that all the trappings and the lifestyle have been obtained fraudulently somehow. With this feeling of being a charlatan, they look for ways to jeopardise it.

Paul Gascoigne is perhaps the best example of this in modern football. I don't want to go into the details of alcoholism, or indeed any other addiction such as drugs or gambling. However, it is interesting to examine how and why this sort of situation can arise.

Harmful behaviours often come from various self-destructive emotions, and one of the most common is anger. Negative emotions make you feel dejected, disempowered and, more importantly, they erode your self-esteem. A sense of inadequacy often gives rise to feelings of guilt, especially if you are idolised by others. It may be that you judge yourself as not living up to the expectations of certain people. Burdened with such emotions, you are likely to need a release from the position you hold.

When Gascoigne was at school, he was walking home with the younger brother of a friend when the boy was tragically hit by a car and killed. The young Gascoigne saw everything. Could the anger about life's unfairness, or even attaching blame to himself, have helped create his later self-destructive tendencies? If that anger had to be suppressed, wouldn't it have come out later in some way? Gascoigne developed a nervous tic soon after the incident.

The problem arises if we don't deal with issues that cause us great discomfort, if we try to avoid them (especially as a young player) by indulging in an activity that overwhelms them. It's the logic of the ostrich. Bad behaviours can be a little like putty – we squeeze it and it simply comes out in other areas.

As problems increase, it can become harder to fix them. We find it easier to justify our bad behaviours than to change them. And don't forget, change can be a scary thing, particularly in the context we're discussing here, where the bad habit exists to cover something we don't wish to expose or deal with. If we're not careful, it ends up being a vicious circle which becomes harder and harder to break out of.

So, I would say the key to continued achievement at a young age is a sense of purpose. People who perform at optimum levels have an excellent understanding of purpose and, more importantly, realise that it is never fully achieved – it's attained again and again on a daily basis.

Targets and objectives can help you on your way to success. In fact, they are extremely useful at driving successful actions. However, targets and objectives are usually numerical. Numbers and metrics work to a certain extent, but having purpose is different gravy. In my experience, in business and sport, you can't beat someone with purpose. The reason why Tiger Woods, Richard Branson and Warren Buffett keep working is because they realise that purpose is a reason for being, a reason to get out of bed in the morning.

A young player with purpose can go far.

THE SECRET PSYCHOLOGIST INTERRUPTS

You want to perform well? Then commit.

If it's in relation to an action – a tackle, a penalty, a save – it's all about matching decisiveness with commitment. Many professional players actually believe that it is better to commit to the wrong decision and fail than to half commit to the right decision and fail. The outcome is sometimes less important than the commitment with which it was reached.

Think about it. Reticence has never been the major trait of a winner. Indeed, many entrepreneurs I have worked with in business do not, contrary to popular belief, have a ton of ideas, nor are they creative geniuses. They just have one idea and commit fully to it. They have a level of focus and a conviction that drive them on until their endeavour bears fruit.

As a footballer trying to complete a task, it is important to 'ATQ' – that is, 'Ask the Question'. The question is always: 'What is my clear intention?' The answer should always be succinct, direct and authoritative; no more than several words to form a short sentence. In the case of a free-kick, it would be something along the lines of: 'I'm going to bend it like this and it will end up top-left corner.'

Our muscles don't respond very well to ambiguous decision-making. If we are speaking the language of 'ifs', 'buts' and 'maybes', our muscles don't seem to comply with the instruction so well. It's almost as if they are confused. Clear, precise direction seems to create a level of clarity necessary for successful task completion.

The more we can ATQ our tasks beforehand, the more committed we are to the end goal. Imagine the following two inner dialogues as you stand at the top of your run to take a penalty:

'I'd like to go top-right corner, but missed one last week when I went there. If I score this we take the lead with 10 minutes left ... maybe low left. Fuck me, that bruise hurts.

THE SECRET PSYCHOLOGIST:
HOW TO SCORE EVERY PENALTY YOU EVER TAKE

Gary Speed had an interesting technique for taking penalties. If ever you asked him what he thought about when he took a penalty, he would say, 'When I know I'm going to take a penalty I ask myself a question. I put the question on loop but I don't answer it. As I run towards the ball, I'm probably two strides away from kicking it when the answer just pops into my head.' The question that Gary asked himself was: Which way would I run, left or right, to celebrate having scored this goal? So he would see himself being successful before completing a task. This is a useful technique for a couple of reasons:

Firstly, Gary was being motivated by what he was seeking to achieve, not motivated by what he was seeking to avoid. Instead of running at the ball thinking, 'Don't hit it left, don't hit it over the keeper, don't hit the woodwork,' he was thinking success outcomes in completing the task.

Secondly, by repeating this question as a mantra – in almost the same way as meditation works when you repeat a sound you are concentrating on – your inner world is keeping your mind occupied and oblivious to the distractions outside of your task, such as opposing fans, opposing players, negative comments or actions.

Fire it down the middle? Keeper's been good today, mind, he'll be confident.'

Or:

'Top-right corner and powerful.'

Which one do you think narrows the eyes and the attention, and plugs the gaps of self-doubt with the sureness of execution?

You can't guarantee success with commitment. But you can be sure of giving yourself the best chance. If you fail but you feel you weren't compromised by the tyranny of self-doubt or the distraction of vagueness, that's got to be something positive.

I honestly believe that when a player performs well, it is not just a purple patch, good form or a lucky run. It is how the player *can* perform all the time. It's simply that the majority of the time we're being interfered with. Something is getting in the way of how we need to think in order to commit fully to the action.

Loss of confidence causes self-doubt, and leads to over-speculation and distracting dialogue. If the physical ability is still there, then surely the loss of form can only be due to interference? This 'interference theory' is applicable to task completion. If we're not engaging in simple directive thoughts, we're not guiding our muscles accurately. But interference can be countered through commitment, as we saw with TSF's goalkeeping colleague.

Players who perform at the highest level always dot the i's and cross the t's. If it's 20 press-ups, they don't do 19½.

These players are the sort who never 'short-change' their talent. It's the discipline that comes with commitment which maximises talent in this case.

Commitment can be strangely liberating. Once we commit, we focus fully on what we are trying to achieve. It frees us up from distraction.

Think about all the roles you play in your life: father, husband, employee, colleague, brother, son, mentor, friend. Our problem is that we mix them all up. We're playing with our child while on the phone dealing with a work issue; we're listening to our partner's issues while writing an email to a mate about that stag do. When we commit to one of those roles at any given time, we are free to focus – to lose ourselves to that particular role at that moment. Distractions are like a gaming machine in a bar, the ringing bells and flashing lights that catch the corner of your eye and turn your attention.

Try holding your hands wide around your eyes, as if you were holding binoculars, and focusing on something 10 feet away and about the size of a 10-pence piece. Usually, in less than a minute you'll notice other things in the peripheral areas: maybe someone or something moving, or appearing to do so. If you start to bring your hands in until you're just looking with one eye though a narrow aperture, as if holding a telescope the diameter of a pencil, you'll find it easier to focus on that same spot for longer. The narrowing of focus holds your attention.

I am convinced that many obstructions players believe they experience are really instructions telling them to focus harder on the important stuff. It is true that the things that matter most should never be at the mercy of things that matter least. Some players will wonder how they can play well when the air conditioning in their hotel was shit and they didn't sleep well last night, or when they have a toothache. Other players, for example John Terry, never saw these things as obstructions – they saw them as distractions that you are free to choose to be diverted by or not.

Often I will say to players, 'Find your pride.' What I mean by this is, be consistent with your commitment. The best players find a level of commitment that stays constant no matter what the circumstances. I don't know who the goalie is that TSF is referring to, but I could pretty much guess that if his team were 3–0 down with five minutes to go, he'd be approaching the game in the same way he did in the first five minutes. Finding your pride is about doing it in the right way because it's important to you.

My friend is a philosopher, which apparently, according to him, is the worst profession to admit to at a party. If you say you're a magician, everyone will ask you to show them a trick. If you're a philosopher, everyone will ask you about the meaning of life or what is love. He says that the definition of happiness is 'finding something that's more important than you, and devoting yourself to it'.

Commitment is exactly the above statement.

It's easy to just let a game go, or get through the last 10 minutes wishing it was over. But finding your pride is about staying honest to yourself and your teammates. I have seen so many professional golfers throw away the final hole after scoring badly on the 17 that preceded it. But can you imagine how much money could be made by a pro golfer who tried his best every tournament to birdie the 18th, no matter what it meant in terms of the competition?

But it's not just about the money. It's the habit of performing to a high standard that has more long-term benefits. Finding your pride is about doing the right stuff all the time because it counts for something ... always.

I was told that, in training, Sam Allardyce likes to keep an eye on the player who is furthest away from the ball. He can tell a lot about a player's ability and attitude by what he is doing when not in the game and off the ball. I think it's the same when players are losing. It's easy to fight when you are winning. The committed players play to the end with the same focus and energy whether they are winning or losing; but losing and keeping going is the tough one.

Finally, two points that I think are important for every player – just a couple of things to bear in mind, which in the long run might simplify the act of achieving your goals. Even for goalkeepers – who, I agree with TSF, are mad.

1. GOAL-SETTING

Goal-setting is an important aid to performance. Goals should be realistic but should stretch you. In setting goals, some people say that you should focus just on the positive. I don't think that's true. With many players, Gary Cahill being one example, I have them set goals, then identify potential barriers to achieving them and what they would do to navigate the obstacles. By doing this, two things happen: the players get a chance to identify and take pre-emptive action against a barrier or inhibitor; or, alternatively, when faced with an obstacle, they are not blindsided and have already thought about the remedial action.

Another essential element in ensuring your continued journey towards goal completion is to make sure you are rewarding yourself along the way. Many great accomplishments are the result of many small accomplishments. Keep noting the small achievements and give yourself a pat on the back, or a Snickers or a weekend off, for reaching another milestone.

When people come to set goals, they also focus too much on the numerical. I understand the notion that what you can measure you can manage, and that you need to know what a good job looks like. However, I always make sure there are some unquantifiable or arbitrarily measured goals. Such as: 'I am going to ask myself at the end of every game – what did I enjoy about today and what did I learn today?' Your goal is to ask those two questions of yourself 100 per cent of the time. So, if you manage to do that, it's another goal ticked off. You might also try rating games according to how much you enjoyed them, perhaps aiming for a score of over 7/10 for the next three matches.

2. OPEN-MINDEDNESS

Do you get an email from someone, see who it's from and the subject, roll your eyes, sigh, and then open it? We all do.

However, your next decision is flawed. You are now going to read that message through a distorted lens and make a decision influenced by bias and prejudice. People who perform at exceptional levels in business and in sport do not see situations as good or bad; they see things as they are. To make the best decisions, we need the facts, nothing else. As soon as we start interpreting things through our own belief system, we start to lose the clarity of understanding we need to read the situation correctly. Nothing is good or bad, it is what it is.

We do three things with all information that comes our way: we delete, distort and filter according to our own belief system. The sad thing is, we always prove ourselves right even when we are wrong. Whatever your viewpoint on politicians, policemen, BMW drivers, your teammates and unfortunately even yourself – you are wrong, but you will always see the evidence that supports your opinion. How many times have you heard someone say shit like, 'We never beat this lot away', 'I never play well in these conditions', 'This ref always has it in for us'? And guess what happens? The world reflects back; it treats us as we treat it.

I would argue that we do not need to think positively or negatively. We need to think with open minds. To change our outer world, we have to change our inner world. And it is the responsibility of a good teammate to challenge existing and limiting belief systems, and create new ways of viewing the supposed and often made-up evidence.

9. THE SYSTEM

How to beat it and how to improve it

I like to conduct my own experiments on the state of our football nation any time England are playing on TV.

Like many football fans around the country, my default setting when England are playing is negativity. I expect very little and I am never disappointed. When England breezed through their Euro qualifying group stage, I suggested in a column I wrote that some people had been carried away with England's dominance. Those people included Roy Hodgson, who seemed very pleased about beating third-rate international sides.

The manager, who should know better than anybody, must surely have realised that the measure of England's progress since their 2014 Brazil World Cup embarrassment could only come against top opposition. It would come in the friendlies against Spain and France.

In friendlies, both teams are usually going at less than full tilt and are probably a little understrength, so we actually get a good chance to see them showing the brand of football they want to play. For example, Spain would pass the ball until they'd moved an England player out of the way before exploiting the space. And England? To be honest, it was hard to tell. We're still not really sure what our brand of football is, are we? Before the game, Vicente del Bosque, Spain's manager, gave an interview in the *Guardian* in which he claimed that England do not have a style of football anymore. He was spot-on and it shows whenever England play.

The truth of what he said is best shown in the sloweddown conditions of a friendly. In the blood-and-bollock conditions of a competitive game, it's harder to discern that we don't know what we're doing. It just looks like a crap performance. What we see is all there is. We don't think back to the friendly and realise that these players simply haven't been given the instruments for a great performance.

When Spain played England in that friendly, I settled back in my seat at home to watch the inevitable unfold. Spain fielded a side with a smattering of world-class talent and some very capable understudies in various other positions. They knew what they were doing. Spain battered England. It was embarrassing.

I tried to snap myself out of it at times; out of the negativity. It can be easy to fall into a trance watching Spain pass the ball about; some people call it boring, which is fine. Those people don't understand football at this level. Mainly because in England we aren't exposed to it much.

It looks as if nothing much is going on, but there is intention in every pass and I'll give you a great example. Andrés Iniesta has the ball in his own half, facing his full-back; he passes him the ball and the full-back gives it back to him. Iniesta is about 15 yards away; he passes to his full-back again and jogs very slowly towards him. Again, he gets the ball back with one touch. It looks pointless.

But what is actually happening is that the whole England team are sliding, subconsciously, towards him as a unit. The closest England player, Fabian Delph, who plays like a typical dog-on-heat English player, breaks ranks and goes towards the ball; and with one final pass to his full-back, Iniesta jogs towards him and then spins as Delph gets within striking distance. The full-back plays it to Iniesta's safe side and suddenly that little backwards-and-forwards, pointless-looking short-passing routine has completely taken Delph out as he hares towards the ball, and Spain are now on the attack.

The England players have been watching this, mesmerised, while the other Spainish players have been getting themselves into position to attack once Iniesta spins – they know it's coming. The Barcelona player switches the ball to Cazorla, who has taken up a dangerous inside-left position, and he in turn plays it to an advanced full-back who has pushed right on to Kyle Walker, who doesn't want to defend anyway. Six little one-touch passes back and forth have affected an entire international team. It is so clever that it is almost impossible for us mortals to do. Spain are dangerous because they are dictating play from seemingly innocuous areas of the pitch, places from which teams think that they cannot possibly come under attack.

I tell myself not to be negative; after all, I'm enjoying Spain's performance because I know by now what clever, intelligent football looks like. And I tell myself that there is a reason why England haven't tried to replicate this football – it is because they can't work out what it is they ought to be replicating.

A dozen years have gone by, Spain have won three international competitions, Barcelona have dominated Europe, and still England's coaches have no idea how Andrés Iniesta, and before him Xavi Hernández, are doing what they do. Our national style is basically no style. We play whatever comes into our head, changing from match to match, using players out of position and hoping for the best.

Maybe I just share the national negativity bias where England are concerned, but it's only because I realise how far away from the likes of Spain we still are, and what really frustrates me is that we have wasted these last dozen years; we have learned nothing. We keep producing the type of players English fans want to see – quick wingers who can't control the football, have little end product and who treat the ball like an unexploded bomb. We want battering rams for strikers, and midfielders pretending to be comfortable on the ball but who come under fire for not taking Iniesta out at the kneecaps.

To be successful you don't even have to innovate; you can imitate and modify. But we are too stupid and too arrogant for that. We did the football Brexit long before the real one. Since Barcelona and Spain unveiled tiki-taka football roughly a dozen years ago, the Germans have found the time to copy it and develop it by adding some Teutonic brute force and blistering counterattacking football into the mix. That adaptation brought the Germans their fourth World Cup triumph in 2014.

Over the same period of time England have learned nothing. Zilch. There has been absolutely no attempt whatsoever to take even one element of any part of Spain's or Germany's model. I really mean that. I see no development in our international game today from what I first watched in the 1986 World Cup. In fact, from a technical standpoint, it could be argued that some of the current crop of players are worse.

But before we blame the players, we should ask where exactly is their blueprint? In France at Euro 2016, nobody seemed to know. Ditto in Brazil in 2014. How does the FA set about drawing up a plan that ensures England win the World Cup in 2022, as the FA's former chairman Greg Dyke pledged?

Do you have any idea how long it takes to produce a player of Iniesta's quality? The concentration that Iniesta needs in order to do what he does, in order to dictate the positions of opposition players and still manipulate the ball with that level of dexterity, is extraordinary. It took him years to learn it, and he learned it from the players who went before him at Barcelona and the coaches who began teaching it to him on his first day at La Masia academy.

A few years ago, Barcelona beat Levante 4–0 in a La Liga game. It was interesting to note that from the 14th minute, when Dani Alves was replaced by Martín Montoya, all the Barça players were graduates of La Masia: Valdés, Montoya, Puyol, Piqué, Alba, Xavi, Busquets, Iniesta, Pedro, Messi, Fàbregas. Not too shabby.

My primary interest in this area of football is the work that goes into finding these kids; after all, there is cause and effect at play here. But you might be surprised to learn that in England, where garnering tomorrow's superstars is concerned, technical talent isn't always the factor by which success is measured. Talent comes in many forms.

As I've mentioned, I came to professional football late. (My talents were Messi-like from an early age, of course, but the system just didn't appreciate me.) I missed out on a few years but I have never regretted it. The first thing that struck me when I went out training with the so-called hardened professionals was how one-sided many of them were. And a lot of them had the touch of a nervy elephant.

Who had been coaching these guys?

Well, these stats from 2013 might help answer that question; and I see no evidence that things have changed much since then.

- At the end of that year, England had 1,178 UEFA 'A' level coaches. Spain had 12,270. Germany had 5,500.
- At the Pro Licence level, England had 203 coaches. Spain had 2,140. Germany had more than 1,000.

- To acquire a UEFA A licence, a coach in England could expect to pay up to £5,820. His German counterpart would spend 530 euros. The Spaniard 1,200 euros.

And before players even reach the coaches, they have to come through the scouts.

A former manager of mine, who had enjoyed some success in the game, then received a thorough kicking from the same game. He regrouped. He took a break and then went back to what he was good at in the beginning: scouting.

He virtually vanished from sight for a couple of years, went underground, and began wearing an anorak instead of a sharp suit. The lines were muddy; there was no baying crowd behind him and no millionaires on the pitch in front of him. He suffered the motorway miles and the wet afternoons of shivering. He pissed into hedges, and when somebody offered him a cup of hot tea it cheered him more than any match bonus.

And when he was ready, when he had learned what he needed to learn, he came back.

From the outside, it might seem like an odd thing to have done, but I guarantee that no club worth its salt would have asked him at a job interview what the fuck he thought he had been doing. Having a breakdown? Creating his own witness protection programme?

No.

Not any club worth its salt, anyway. But there are fewer of those in England than you might think.

In theory, good scouting is important to every club. In practice, it is important only to the far-sighted. When the suits in the accounts office want to make a few snips, the scouting network and the academy facilities are the easy target. Maybe a few dinner ladies too, or chefs, as we call them now.

Scouting and good coaching should be elemental to good clubs these days. The more we talk about things like deadline-day madness, the more worthwhile decent scouting becomes. If we don't have a scouting structure, or don't pay any more than lip service to that structure, we would be better off going back to the era of street football and looking for those kids who don't really exist anymore, the kids who score 120 goals a year because nobody has ever coached it out of them and stuck them into the straitjacket of some system that nobody believes in. I mean, it doesn't matter how many goals Cristiano Ronaldo may score, there are many people in English football who proudly boast that they wouldn't have him in their team. He doesn't track back, see.

Finding players and putting them in contact with good coaches in a system that will reward them with first-team presence is the key to developing the game nationally. Yet in all clubs scouts are still poorly paid, under-appreciated and generally sopping wet. And the more commercially worthwhile it becomes to have decent scouts, the more open the whole ancient system becomes to crooks and scam artists. The men who have basically done the job for the love of it, while surviving by holding down a real job 40 or 50 hours a week, are being elbowed aside by the Mister 10 Per Cent types.

A manager who knows the scene, and who knows which players have genuine value and which are overhyped dross, is invaluable. So too is a manager who knows which voices from among the chorus of scouts telling him who to sign are worth listening to.

You get a kid, say a Marcus Rashford, who is toiling away with the youths one day and at the European Championship just days later – straight away you have covered the cost of a couple of years' scouting and your academy. Rashford joined Manchester United as a nine-year-old from Fletcher Moss Rangers in Didsbury. That's the same club which coughed up Tyler Blackett, Danny Welbeck, Ravel Morrison, Wes Brown and others. The funny thing is that Manchester City dithered over signing Rashford because, at nine, he seemed a bit on the small side.

They won't make the same mistake again. I read a piece recently in which Sheffield United scout Luke Fedorenko lamented losing a pair of 11-year-olds to Manchester City. It's not so long since Fedorenko was the bright young thing himself at Barnsley, and there were constant rumours of Premier League interest. It didn't happen and he ended up at university instead, studying sports science. He's well qualified to assess the odds of those two 11-year-olds making it to the other end of the system at City.

It's not like being at La Masia. City will never, ever field a team full of its academy graduates. The loss aversion is too strong. Buy an international for 40 million and stick him in there. Buy a shedload of them. Get into Europe. Recoup the cash. Job done. That's the English way.

In England, even though the top leagues haven't grown in size, the number of English-born players in those leagues has consistently shrunk. Scouting is like a latter-day gold rush for clubs who are smart enough to know what one decent nugget can mean. Manchester United have over 80 scouts working the north-east region alone. Unfortunately, as the figures above show, our coverage of decent coaches is so poor that we are sifting through substandard soil most of the time.

Fans love a homegrown hero (till he leaves and becomes an instant Judas), but clubs love a conveyor belt of talent that can be sold on. Look at clubs like Porto, Udinese or Southampton – the leaders in the field at buying and selling. They are sustainable because they scout well. And they'll listen to any phone call from a buying club that is wealthy enough.

Even clubs like Chelsea, who provide minimal opportunity for progress to the first team, will spend £10m or so a year on their youth academy. They get a stream of decent players who are not quite good enough to muscle their way into the first team (what manager would be allowed to break a kid in at Stamford Bridge when he has the money to buy the finished article whenever he wants?) and so generally get sent on for needless minutes.

This is all short-termism driven by commercial needs. It contributes virtually nothing to the health of English football. The fact is that the science of finding and developing under-age talent has lagged well behind the greed of the system it serves. Football is only now catching up on the science side of things. English football at the top level doesn't care. How many seriously good players, meanwhile, have been lost to the game through ignorance?

Crusty old scouts used to ask, 'What is potential?' A couple of arms and a couple of legs, they'd say. Clubs today need more than that. There are scouts out there watching kids who are five or six years old. They are looking for the earliest signs of speed, touch, co-ordination, balance and footballing intelligence. And a bit of confidence. And they are narrowing the opportunities for those kids at the same time.

There have certainly been changes to the system compared to how it operated even 10 or 15 years ago. In fact, it has become unrecognisable. The question is whether the system, even if it does make money for club owners, is better for young players and for the English game as a whole. Is it even right? Professor Ross Tucker, the South African sports scientist, described the entire system as a 'race to the bottom'. It is a quote that I love and hate in the same breath.

One damning stat gave weight to Tucker's colourful phrase. There are 12,500 players currently in the English academy system and only 0.5 per cent of the under-nines at top clubs will ever make it to the first team. If you happen to be nine years old, then you're looking at odds of 200–1. Worse still, the drop-out rate for the game in the 13–16-year-old age group is around 76 per cent, similar to rugby union.

The report included a great quote from Nick Levett, who is an expert in the development of players in the 8–11-year-old age group: 'Anyone who tells you they can spot a professional player at five years old is basically lying.' Nick's blog, Rivers of Thinking, is a stream of useful information which any parent and any young player should familiarise themselves with. Not to mention any youth coach.

Leaving aside the struggles that an ordinary kid has to improve his game, he has to contend with the flaws in a system that spreads its nets wide but doesn't know what sort of fish it is looking for. First, there is the Matthew effect. Many people first came across this concept in Malcolm Gladwell's book *Outliers*, in which the eponymous chapter begins with the biblical quote from Matthew that gives the phenomenon its name: 'For unto everyone that hath shall be given, and he shall have abundance. But from him that hath not shall be taken away even that which he hath.'

For kids in sports this means that the system sets out with a false definition of what a good young player is, the system then adjusts its behaviour accordingly and the original false definition ends up looking valid. And this starts on the day your child is born. In Canadian hockey, the cut-off for age groups at youth level is 1 January. If your little darling is born on 2 January or close to it, when he turns 10 he could be skating against kids who won't turn 10 until 10 or 11 months later. Generally, he'll be bigger and better developed than those kids. He'll catch the eye more. He'll get picked for the elite teams. He'll get the better coaching. He'll play more games.

If the system decides that it knows how to separate the 'talented' from the 'not-so-talented' at an early age, it rewards the 'talented' with so much extra opportunity and coaching that the initial judgement call seems to justify itself. After a few years, the kid getting all the coaching and games will be genuinely better than the kid who doesn't receive all those benefits. It stands to reason.

In England, the cut-off date in football is 31 August. According to Nick Levett's blog, 57 per cent of the players in Premier League academies are born in the months September, October and November. Just 14 per cent are born in the summer months at the end of the football year, June, July and August. A few years ago, Levett studied a Surrey junior league with 8,000 players. He found that division one in all age groups had the oldest players on average. Division seven had the youngest. Of course they did.

Guess which division the scouts generally paid attention to.

It's called relative age bias. The irony is that a smaller kid born in the wrong month can beat the system; he will probably benefit hugely from having to battle harder than everybody else. Someday, the physical advantages will even out and he will be a better player perhaps than the bigger kid who got things easier. A small kid has to keep working harder and being smarter. The very things we value greatly in senior players. Clubs are only just beginning to see that.

It levels out in the end, but clubs are slow learners. The biggest drop-out rates among 13–15-year-olds in football are among those kids born in the third and fourth quarters of the year, from March to August.

Jamie Vardy is the perfect example. Sheffield Wednesday cut him loose when he was 16 years old because he was too small. He was lucky in one way. He managed to hang on, on the fringes of the system. Seven years with Stocksbridge Park Steels. Not the stuff of dreams. Nobody noticed his talent. A year with Halifax Town. A year with Fleetwood. Finally, Leicester City came in for him and you know the rest. Hollywood want to make his life into a movie, but personally I'd be more interested in a documentary about how the system missed him. What were all the biases that kept Jamie Vardy down?

Perhaps Vardy suffered from what is known as the unconscious bias. We'll come on to this in more detail later, but it is basically the tendency of scouts and coaches to make up their mind very early on about what they think of a player, and for everything they see after that point to be filtered through their prejudice so that it confirms the bias.

Levett tweeted a good example of this during the European Championship: he pointed out that if Olivier Giroud missed a chance, analysts agreed that this was proof of the fact that he wasn't quite top class, but if his French teammate Antoine Griezmann missed a chance he was simply 'unlucky'. In the end, Griezmann scored more goals, but Giroud's contribution was still significant. And give Griezmann a year or two in England and our footballing negativity would have his confidence back to the level it was as a teen, when clubs routinely rejected him for being too small.

Football lore is full of the stories of players who almost fell through the net because they didn't fit the bias of a scout. Zinedine Zidane was a tough and troubled kid who signed for Cannes when the club's director asked him to come and live with his family. He found some sort of equilibrium there. They encouraged him to channel his anger into football. Eric Cantona flirted with not being that lucky – until Alex Ferguson took him in, no club wanted the man. Stan Collymore nearly slipped through. Ditto Robin van Persie.

And then there are all the guys that we professionals knew at some stage. The guys who were dead certs to make it. They're working in factories now some of them. Others are taking drugs. Plenty more are selling them. Others went and got an education and forgot about the dream entirely.

They haunt us.

A player aged 13 or 14 can get a reputation for being temperamental or lazy or slow and that will be his footballing epitaph. One scout says to the other that the winger looks handy. The second scout replies that maybe he is, but he is lazy. First scout nods and makes a mental note: Lazy.

Two lazy examples of 'what you see is all there is' syndrome, resulting in consigning a player to the scrapheap. And you can't be lazy. Not if you are going to change the health of English football.

Malcolm Gladwell also popularised the 10,000-hour theory, the notion that any donkey can be turned into a thoroughbred just by clocking up 10,000 hours of practice. This will seem odd to any of us who were in school with kids who were just outrageously talented at everything but not really arsed about working hard at anything. They were better for a different reason.

The 10,000-hour theory also led to a culture of parents virtually attaching meters to their children's backs so that they could monitor how far away the mythical 10,000-hour mark was. Ten thousand hours? Give me a fucking break. But it's a great idea for a book. It appeals to the innermost voice residing in many of us that whispers, 'I can be a professional footballer, I can!'

The 10,000-hour theory is dead. The latest craze is the search for myelin, a white matter that in optimal conditions grows as part of the infrastructure of the brain and accelerates the traffic in the mind. As Daniel Coyle says in *The Talent Code*, 'Myelin has the capacity to regulate velocity, speeding or occasionally even slowing signals so they hit the synapses at the optimal time ... nerve firings grow myelin, myelin controls impulse speed and impulse speed is skill.' Myelin growth is prompted by deep practice, but at the right times and in the right conditions. And myelin can't be spotted by men in anoraks standing on muddy sidelines, and nor can it be injected by parents living their dreams through their kids.

Kids have to get past all these hurdles of bias and misinformation. And then there is the problem at the heart of the system: the rewards. A player who has grown up within the system can find himself as an 18-year-old earning £20k a week before bonuses. Damien Comolli, who has worked as a scout and with scouts at a range of top clubs, points out that players growing up in this cocoon can often be soft: 'Most have a comfortable life and environment and those two things fail to produce players who need to fight every day on the field. If you look at attacking players at the top 20 or 30 teams across Europe, many are from South America. From a mental aspect, they have a greater drive.'

He may be right about the drive of South American players, but I would argue that the top teams in Spain and Germany produce an abundance of their own players who will go on to wear the Spanish or German national jersey. And they have the drive and skill to thrive in the system they have been taught in.

The English system just grinds on meanwhile, slowly developing an awareness that the way things have always been done might not be the best way to always do things.

We've come a long way from 'the two arms and two legs' theory of potential. And we have just as far to go. In England, we have barely started the journey, but don't worry, it's the greatest league in the world, remember, and the FA says we will win the World Cup in 2022.

2022? We'll be happy to make par.

THE SECRET PSYCHOLOGIST INTERRUPTS

TSF poses some questions above about talent and how we in England find it and treat it.

There are two types of talent: 'talent that shouts' and 'talent that whispers'. Lots of people can see the talent that shouts. The talented youngster who seems head and shoulders above the rest. The lad who lives and breathes his sport and technically, psychologically, physically outguns all the others in the group. Their talent is obvious and they get invested in and courted by many interested parties.

The talent that whispers is the interesting one. This is where clubs can make great gains. It's the lad who does all right; he has good tactical and technical ability and every now and then plays a blinder.

As scouts, it is possible to get blinded by formulaic criteria and habitual thinking. Even our own ego can cause an unhelpful bias in determining accurately a player's real ability and value. Wouldn't it be great to sign the next big thing? Or discover the next international phenomenon?

I take the stance that as a business or as an individual, our only sustainable competitive advantage is to learn faster and better than our competitors. The talent that whispers knows this too. They may not be the best, but they have an unseen advantage – the ability and willingness to learn. Not only do they immerse themselves in their craft, but they spend time engaging in 'experiential learning'. David Beckham was an experiential learner. He would practise free-kicks and make minor adjustments to his weight distribution or body positioning to see what happened as a result. Imagine practising 30 free-kicks from some distance out, and breaking them down into sets of six, and on each set you leaned a little further back than normal. Just by observing the result, it would tell you a little more about the connection between your body and the outcome.

This gamification of practice allows us to understand and subconsciously translate the relationship between subtle shifts in physical stance and the end result in a fun and practical way. Playing the game of 'what if?' is an important way to learn for the talent that whispers.

In fact, 'playing' in general is an essential element of success for such a quiet talent. Many people believe they have to work hard. Work is not a pleasant word, and conjures up an image of toil and endeavour. The talented performer knows that being better comes from having fun and ensuring there is a maintained level of enthusiasm. This comes from seeing improvement as an enjoyable challenge; playing at getting better.

Think about every professional footballer kicking a ball for the first time as a kid. The fun was not in winning or being paid well. It was in doing five keepy-uppies and having a right laugh with your mates as you try to get to 10. There was massive self-satisfaction and achievement in getting to six. Improvement was quick and steep at such a young age, due not just to the hours put in, but to the energy and mindset which underpinned the practice.

It is estimated that, in our entire lifetime, we learn the most between the ages of one and three. Not only is this incredibly sad, but it is also fairly obvious. When you think about everything that you know how to do now – eating with a knife and fork, walking, talking, in fact everything – you have learned how to do it through repeated failure. We have been born necessarily imperfect. When you look at infants aged one to three, you can see that all they do is spend the day repeatedly failing – doing a thing to a particular standard and then having fun trying to better it.

The talent that whispers knows that the competition is himself, and he plays the game of getting better by understanding his talent. Through experiential learning, immersion and self-awareness, the kid with average talent starts to outperform the kid with the ability but not the mindset.

There are also players who are like a slow-burning firework. The type with 'permanent potential', always on the brink of something special but never quite achieving it. They glow without ever catching flame, and you think that's it – then boom! They take off. Having been released by a few clubs and in and out of contracts, they're suddenly flying high and shining brightly, that label of 'permanent potential' well and truly gone.

I think scouts need to look beyond the obvious.

A study carried out in the Canadian girls' ice hockey leagues tried to understand why some girls were higher performers than others. It actually had nothing to do with the month they were born in or the hours they practised or their educational triumphs. The only correlation between the best players turned out to be how many times they fell over. The girls who performed at the highest level had more falls than their less successful counterparts when learning new moves. Now, if you were scouting, it's not as easy as saying that you should be looking for a player who hits the ice a lot. She may actually just be shit. My point is that a certain type of fall may be a tick in the box. If the player is falling because she is testing the extremes of the move, or pushing herself towards an area of opportunity which exists outside of normal performance, then it might just say something about her mindset.

It's the same in football. Someone who is testing and trying, and even losing or making mistakes as a result, might just be finding the correct balance of attitude to maximise their talent.

10. WHEN TIMES GET TOUGH

Transferred to the pit of despair

Since England won the World Cup back in the Middle Ages, who are the three greatest British natural talents to have graced our leagues? You could argue forever but Best, Gazza and Rooney would be hard to leave out of any top five. And we destroyed them. We laughed at them, not with them. We stuck a pin through those butterflies and we pinned them to a board and watched them flap their gorgeous wings as they died. Ha ha.

We used to say, 'Oh, it was the papers, the media, the tabloids' – as if those organs would have thrived without us feeding them our attention. And we look at pictures of Gazza now and say, 'Oh, it's so sad, look at the state of him. Somebody should do something.' I agree. You should have done something 30 years ago, like changing your newspaper.

We live in the age of Twitter now, where everybody has an opinion and everybody feels that everybody else is entitled to that opinion no matter how shit and wrong it is. And we see ourselves reflected in our social media: overwhelmingly negative and giant whingers. That is what we are.

People write on Twitter about footballers who have made the same mistakes in life that just about everybody else has. But the words being used are along the lines of 'disgusting', 'despicable', 'scumbag', 'appalling human being', 'total prick'. The consensus is that these overpaid, pampered, ungrateful scumbag bastards don't realise just how lucky they are. If the tweeter in question had enjoyed the sheer luck to be that young, talented and rich, then *he* would have used his powers for good; he would have used the afternoons after training to work tirelessly to eliminate world poverty and cure cancer.

And of course it is only bad luck that stopped the embittered tweeter from being not just a world-class player but a world-class humanitarian too.

Bullshit.

One of my favourite studies illustrates how other people's responses affect an individual's performance. A few years back, a psychologist at Columbia University by the name of Carol Dweck put together a study to examine how praise affected the performance of students. The results were surprising.

Dweck's research team conducted their experiments on 400 fifth-graders. First, they took the students away from their classrooms and gave them each a non-verbal IQ test. The test was pretty easy and naturally most of the kids did well in it. That was the point.

The important bit came when the test had been completed. When the kids received their scores, they were told one of two things:

'Well, you must be smart.'
Or:
'You must have worked really hard.'

The next day the students were tested again, except this time they were asked to choose between two tests: one test was more difficult than the first one they'd done; the other test was just as easy. The researchers found that the kids who had been praised for being smart generally opted to take the easy test, while those who had been praised for their hard work almost always chose the more difficult test.

Being praised for effort seemed to motivate the students more than being praised for some kind of natural intelligence. That's the core of it. When people think about Mozart, Einstein, Bill Gates, Mark Zuckerberg, Steve Jobs or me, they usually think how smart those people are, not how hard they worked. When people think of great footballers, they tend to think how lucky they were to come out of the womb able to play football. The reality is that players who end up in the Premier League worked like dogs all their lives to get there. Even the 'natural talents'. Scratch the surface and you will always find a kid who lived through football, who spent hour upon hour trying out things and perfecting them.

We feel better about ourselves if we preserve the illusion that certain individuals got to the top because they possessed something that other people didn't – some sort of genius or innate talent. The truth in almost every case is that endurance, perseverance, work ethic and passion for what they did were what separated them from the herd. As Gary Player once said, 'The harder I work, the luckier I get.'

Carol Dweck's study showed that kids who were praised for being 'smart' didn't push themselves to achieve as much as they might have because they believed that intelligence alone would let them coast to success. This belief that you are smart or just talented causes people to fear failure from early on, and so those people take fewer risks and don't accomplish and learn in the way that the hard-working kids do.

Cristiano Ronaldo again. He's narcissistic, arrogant, selfish and easy to dislike. Not like that cuddly little tax evader, Messi. Talk to anybody who has ever played with him, though, and they'll tell you Ronaldo worked harder than anybody they have ever seen. And still does. And so do Messi, Suárez, Zlatan and so on down to my friend, the old foreign goalkeeper. Hard work applies to just about any great player you care to mention. Not working, treading water, deciding that you have done enough, those are the things that get you into trouble. Ask Mario Balotelli.

So let's stop resenting young players and the money they earn purely because they are so good that we will pay subscriptions just to be able to watch them. They didn't make the world they live in. You did.

And it's not an easy world. Here's a headfuck for you. I have a mate who is a professional snooker player. When he was younger, much younger, he won every tournament that he entered and he was tipped as a future world champion.

Nobody talks about him like that anymore.

Snooker is a mental game. Sure, it's also skilful and technical and tactical, but it's a hugely psychological game. When my friend turned professional, he told me that the standard of play was brutal. Now, that isn't a word you'd associate with snooker, and when I pressed him on it the answer was not what I expected.

He told me that the game of snooker at the highest level breaks two ways: you play the balls, and you also play the mind of the other man. Every player on the circuit can play the balls. That's a given. Whoever can get into the mind of the other player in the most effective way during the contest usually wins the tight matches.

My friend told me that when players take a shot into the corner pocket behind which their opponent is sitting, the only thing you can see moving is the eyes of the other player. I've since studied this and it is amazing how many times the player who is sitting down flicks his eyes up to the sky just as the shot is about to be taken. My friend said that when it first happened it was the most off-putting thing he'd ever seen. The more he tried not to think about it, the more he thought about it.

Other forms of psychological warfare include thumping the table; banging the cue on the floor; deliberately slowing down the play to aggravate another player who has just missed an easy shot; staying down on the shot that you know was difficult in order to milk the applause; staying at the table when it's not your shot just to admire a safety shot that you have just played; and sitting bolt upright and following the other player around the room with your eyes in order to intimidate him (apparently Peter Ebdon was very good at this).

My friend couldn't deal with the psychological battles. On the elite circuit, his game just deteriorated. But as so often happens when you're involved in sport at this level, you spot a lifeboat. You grab on to any old ex-player, or any person with some kind of knowledge about the game, who you hope will slip a magic bullet into your sweaty palm. I call these people 'chancers'. Other people call them gurus.

My friend met a man who claimed that he could improve his game dramatically. He'd watched him and he had the solution. He told my friend that his alignment was out and that he wasn't delivering the cue in a straight line; he told him that his stance was too high, which meant he was digging down too much and imparting a little trace of side on to the cue ball, which was throwing it off line and causing him to miss shots.

In my friend's head, this all made sense. Snooker players are like golfers and tennis players. When things are bad they'll listen to any sort of advice of this nature. And the chancer-cum-guru was right in a way. Those things do happen to snooker players and it can affect their game. So my friend threw a lot of money at the problem – and what happened? He got worse. And by that point he was 25 and going nowhere; his chance was gone. He had a great future behind him.

He had been beaten by the inability to cope with the mental pressures at the top of his favourite game. Obviously he bought into the technician's advice because it was easier to think that the cure lay in working hard and working smarter. The cure wasn't physical, though, it was mental, and it took my friend too long to believe it.

And, of course, it isn't just snooker. Phil Taylor, the 16-time world darts champion, once told me excitedly that he had been approached by a firm in Holland that specialised in aerodynamic arrows. Their pitch was nothing more complex than the suggestion that they couldn't believe that the arrows the great Phil Taylor had been throwing for all of those years were the shape of biscuit tins. Imagine how good he could be with these new, never-before-seen, Nobel Prize-winning aerodynamic darts that nobody else had!

They had jumped on Phil shortly after he'd lost a World Championship final, ignoring the fact that the arrows he'd been using with all the aerodynamics of a biscuit tin had won him all of his world titles and that this was due in no small part to the fact that he was completely at ease with their weight and feel, having used them for 20-odd years. But all Phil saw was the chance to go to another level. After all, who doesn't want to get better and better? Phil saw the world title he'd just lost, not the 16 that he'd actually won. Losses weigh heavier with us than wins, remember?

I don't think he has won the world title since. The mind can be a bugger sometimes.

The point I am making is that there are psychological problems to overcome at every turn as a professional sportsperson, whether you're young or old and regardless of what sport you're part of. When players don't perform to the extremely high level that we expect of them, take a moment to remember all those who didn't have the work ethic or the mentality to get that far in the first place. And remember the deficiencies of the system in which they have grown up and now work.

The blazers who create the environment for English footballers to grow in generally don't know what they are doing, and when they do know, the job is too big for them anyway. Knowing that is the first mental hurdle for a lot of players. You realise that half the people who are in your ear or on your training ground believe that you have been throwing biscuit tins and that they are the first ever to have come up with the idea of aerodynamics.

So, as the Secret Psychologist taught us, ATQ – Ask the Question. Who is going to make you better? Who is going to see the things you do well and the things you do badly and not apply a halo effect to one and a pitchfork effect to the other?

That's a huge mental hurdle. And it's apart from the money, the pressure, the hangers-on and the fact that nobody prepared your brain for all that. And those mental hurdles come at you from a young age. And you try to jump them with millions of people watching you. Mostly people who have no idea of the circumstances and context within which those hurdles are found.

There are so many reasons why good youngsters don't make it.

In my view, young players are removed from their comfort zone (i.e. their mothers) at far too early an age. At the critical juncture in their life when they need the back-bone of their family and the sanctuary of a home to fall back on, they can suffer enormously from feelings of loneliness and social isolation.

George Best was so desolate in digs in Manchester that he and his friend did a runner back to Belfast. Leave aside the social demographics and the gulf between the kids who are 'haves' and the kids who 'have-a-lot-fucking-less' and you find that fear, isolation and a constant feeling of worthless-ness are the drivers that force kids off the rails.

From 1960, the American psychologist Harry Harlow began publishing his findings from a set of experiments relat-ing to maternal separation and social isolation. He did this by comparing how baby monkeys reacted to a warm, fluffy-looking monkey made of cloth that served no purpose whatso-ever against a loud, metal, aggressive-looking monkey made of wire that offered food to the baby monkey. Harlow observed that the comfort of physical contact and the reassurance of just feeling safe actually usurped the basic requirements of survival where the baby monkey was concerned. They preferred the fluffy, useless monkey.

We haven't evolved as far from the monkeys as we like to think we have.

I was in my late twenties when I secured a move for some millions to a Premier League club. That club handed me a wage somewhere north of £30,000 a week. I could buy everything I had ever wanted. I had the status, the reputation, the lot. I had officially made it.

There was one problem: I had to move away from everything that I knew. My home, my extended family, my friends and my old life. My wife had to do the same, but she had to do it with a newborn baby. She knew nobody when we arrived in our new home. She knew nobody when we left it a year later with our monkey tails between our legs.

It was a disaster for us both. During that whole time, in those rare moments when we actually talked to each other, we wished and prayed that we could be delivered back to the place where we had felt loved, and safest. Nobody outside of myself and Mrs TSF knew what was going on. People simply saw a player who wasn't succeeding in the way they thought he would.

We needed reassurance and comfort from somebody we could trust and love. We both needed to have people around us who cared about us unconditionally, people who couldn't have cared less how the football was going. And I needed better support at the club. The manager who loved me on the afternoon of transfer deadline day decided that he didn't love me anymore. His attitude was that it wasn't him, it was me. I wanted to work as hard as I had ever worked. I wanted to play and do well. He wasn't interested.

I think of that period any time I see a lynch mob of those without sin gathering up stones and queuing to be the first to throw those stones at some kid who isn't making it.

Remember Kahneman? What you see is all there is. You are making up a narrative without knowing the facts.

Harlow had shown us all this stuff about home and security many years earlier but, controversially, he would go further. In his later experiments, which he called 'the pit of despair', baby monkeys were left alone in darkness for up to one year from birth, separated from their peers and isolated in the 'pit' at random times. These experiments produced monkeys that were severely psychologically disturbed. Harlow then moved on to his psychiatric phase by attempting to treat the monkeys back to health. He failed.

Today I am forced to consider what the effects must have been on my son as I chased money, possessions and my own stupid legacy. All the while, I was dragging us deeper into our own pit of despair. I was hard to live with, hard to be around. Superficially, I had succeeded – look at my bank account – but I knew that on the hierarchy of human needs I was a long way from fulfilment and happiness. And worse, deep down I had always sensed that this wasn't the club for me.

I can't apologise for the morbidity of this chapter because it's all fact. I'm afraid that the world doesn't run on love. Lift the lid on football and it is a cruel, selfish, ruthless little world. There are moments that fool you into believing that the dream is actually your reality, and you learn to grab those moments. For the rest of the world, those moments are all that anybody sees.

As young footballers, we all had it ingrained into our souls to be as successful as possible and to chase the dream until we reached our peak and had gone as far as we could go. Whatever that level is, and whenever it might come, you are obliged to get to it. Nobody tells you to find the level at which you are happy and challenged and fulfilled. Nobody warns you that if you make it to the professional ranks, success and happiness aren't necessarily part of the deal.

The truth is that the life of a player is littered with rejections at every turn. Most youth-team players are rejected completely, and most youth-team players who turn professional in the Premier League are then rejected by those clubs. They move on to lower-league clubs where they kind of start again, with people muttering behind their backs that they didn't cut it at United or City or wherever.

By the age of 23, most young players will have been rejected by all levels of professional football completely. The ones who survive in England have worked hard, in a flawed system that pays them well but doesn't know how to get the best out of them.

Depending on where you begin, the life of a footballer will almost always involve a lot of rejection. And it never ends. And when the time comes to retire and you sit in your ivory tower wondering what the fuck you're going to do with the second half of your life, that rejection scratches at the back of your head every day – scratch, scratch, fucking scratch ...

THE SECRET PSYCHOLOGIST INTERRUPTS

Very few sporting careers are just a series of good decisions and correct turns at every fork in the road. Sportspeople can be so focused on success that when they find themselves ambushed by a mistake or a bad decision, their sense of well-being takes a beating into the bargain. Difficulties will arise, and coping with them is part of how you go on to success.

TSF writes about moving to the wrong club. It happens. It is not just the player who suffers as a result of making the wrong decision for the wrong reason. The club does too. And the player's family. In this scenario, what you need to do is find a solution that makes everybody happy. I suspect that, in TSF's case, nobody at his new club saw this.

When you sit in front of a 17-year-old who still lives at home even though he earns £50k a week and he tells you that he wants to kill himself (and you) because he missed that penalty, no textbook will ever give you the answer. There is no easy response. In fact, I managed to make a difference simply by saying to him over a pint in the pub one night, 'Why don't you just stop being a wanker and practise more?'

No psychology degree needed for that! However, what is essential is knowing in each individual case exactly what you should and shouldn't say, and at what moment, to push that person into thinking differently. One thing about the pit of despair: a ladder will always get you out of there. The player in question was a future superstar who was coasting into poor performance. No one gave him a hard time or challenged him with any conviction, which is what he actually needed. That challenge was his ladder out of the pit.

Here's another example: I was working with a cricketer who wanted to gain a central contract; in other words, he wanted to be in the England squad. He put so much pressure on himself that his game was turning to shit. The emotional highs and lows of every moment of every match were exhausting him.

I talked to him. First, I clarified his exact goal. He confirmed that it was to be in the national set-up within two years. I asked him to answer yes or no to the following questions:

Q: If you had a shocker tomorrow, the worst game possible [he was a bowler], could you still be in the England set-up in two years?

A: Yes.

Q: If you had the best game possible tomorrow, could you be selected for the squad in the same timeframe?

A: Yes.

Q: If you learned nothing from now until then, could you be there?

A: No. No way.

Very quickly, he started to realise that long-term gain did not come from short-term success. His goals and his perception of those goals were inhibiting him. The key for him was to learn his way to international cricket. There were bends in a road that he'd hoped might be straight. Each individual game was important, but important in a different way to how he'd perceived it.

That is the way with every career. How we perceive our goals and the perspective we have on our failures can make all the difference.

11. THE MIND'S EYE

The art of visualisation

In the mid-sixties, the famed American psychologist Eckhard Hess ran an experiment in which male volunteers were asked to look at photographs of women's faces and make judgements on them. Hess placed two photographs side by side of the same woman in the same pose and the volunteers had to note which picture they preferred. The only subtle difference between the pictures was that one had been retouched slightly. The pupils appeared dilated in one picture but remained unchanged in the other.

It is widely known nowadays that when a woman's pupils are dilated it is a sign, among other things, that she is sexually aroused. None of the men back then noticed that there was any difference in pupil size between the two pictures and, besides, none of them were aware of what dilated pupils might be signalling.

Overwhelmingly, when asked to choose which picture they viewed most favourably the men went for the one with the dilated pupils.

The men's unconscious awareness had run a series of lightning-quick, deep-rooted evolutionary calculations that had directly influenced their decision without them being at any point consciously aware of it. Eckhard Hess had proven that there are two distinct layers of consciousness: a person is either consciously aware or unconsciously aware.

Years later, Daniel Kahneman took Hess's pupil-dilation work some way further. He found that the mental energy being spent on a task could be measured through pupil dilation. When a person succeeded or just gave up, the pupils shrank back again. Kahneman was thus able to confirm that the more skilled we become at a task, the less mental energy it requires.

How does this apply to a footballer?

Well, with confidence comes control, balance, poise, reaction and swagger. And footballing confidence comes with practice, repetition and successful execution of the task. But footballing intelligence is slightly different. Footballing intelligence involves being able to focus on the execution of the task at hand while also sifting through the options for what happens next. Lots of people can kick a ball well. Not so many can kick it well with precisely the right pace and timing for the ball to arrive in a space into which a player nobody else has noticed is running at full tilt.

In other words, lots of people can drive a car from A to B without really focusing on what they are doing. Not many people could drive the same journey while concentrating intensely on solving mathematical equations. Football at the top level represents the same challenge.

During a football match, the brain is sending out signals all the time to the muscles needed to perform the function required. Goalkeepers need fast reactions, and although these can be improved by coaching, studies have shown that their brains are able to process information faster and as a result they are able to react quicker in order to save shots. In short, and I am reluctant to admit this, these guys are actually goalkeepers for a better reason than the fact that they were too shit as kids to play anywhere else. But they're still mad.

The best example of a sportsman's unconscious awareness in full swing isn't actually to be found within football. Major League Baseball pitchers are among the most highly paid athletes in the world. Their task is to throw baseballs at a batter in a way that minimises his chances of hitting the ball. They have to throw the baseball into an imaginary box that runs from the pitcher's knee to the midpoint of his torso. The strike zone. Passing the ball three times through this small zone without it being hit results in the batter being out. There's more to it, but that is the basis of what you need to know about pitching.

Now consider the batter's task – which is not to hit every ball thrown at him, but to hit the right ball in the right way. To do that, his brain has to perform a series of incredibly complex and lightning-quick analytical processes. Among other things, the batter has to wait for the light to bounce off the white ball and register in his brain through his eyes. Then he has to decide whether the ball is actually coming into the strike zone. If not, there is no need to swing at all. At the same time, his brain has to determine how fast the ball is coming at him and where it is likely to pitch.

Baseballs don't come bouncing up off the crease; they are thrown to pitch in the air. The pitcher might have thrown a fastball, which could come in at a speed of between 95 and 106 mph. It might be a knuckleball, a changeup, a screwball, a curveball or any one of the pitches that will break or pitch violently in the air. The brain then has to send signals to the right muscles for swinging the bat and connecting with the ball. Not connect blindly either. The batter might need to bunt or try a line drive or swing for the fences looking for a home run.

And he has to decide on all this and execute it in slightly less than 0.4 seconds. The batter's conscious awareness simply does not have enough time to register all of those variables and make a decision based on conscious thinking. He is only aware of what has happened after the ball is struck. He has spent a lifetime wiring his brain that way.

This isn't true only of baseball, but of all sports; in fact, in all areas of life. There is a part of your brain that just takes over. But it is possible to train that part of your brain. For example, every time you jump on a bike your subconscious brain takes over. It uses a series of electrical pulses to tell you which leg to swing over the frame, how to grip the handles, when to take your feet off the floor, how fast to go and when to brake, and it does that automatically. The reason we know this is because you can have a conscious conversation with somebody next to you as you do all these things.

Think about your schooldays. You went every day for years, maybe 10 years or so (well, most of you did), and yet not only can you not remember every day, you can't even remember certain years. You might be able to remember some specific moments, but that's about it. And it's not because you got old and forgot; it's because you went through most of those days on autopilot.

When I look back at certain games – well, most games – I don't remember an awful lot about the way they went; I can't even remember some goals that I scored. Once, I gave an interview to a reporter after a game in which I'd managed to score. He noted that it was the perfect start to the game given that my goal had come after two minutes. I asked him to check his facts properly because I was convinced it had come midway through the first half. He was right, and it just goes to show that even in the heat of battle you can go to a place where your natural instincts take over, without you being consciously aware of what's happening around you.

But while your subconscious can achieve things your conscious mind could never dream of, it can also trip you up. There was a time in my career when Arsenal routinely beat us to death. Back then, our manager had a soft spot for Arsenal. He believed they were a team of extremely talented footballers who should be seen as a benchmark for modern-day players to try to emulate. They were everything he thought that we should be. But we weren't. They were the 'My Perfect Cousin' of football. He paid them too much respect and it rubbed off on us. As a result, we became soft when Arsenal rocked up because, subconsciously, we knew that our manager expected us to get beat. We tried only so hard to win.

During one particular game, Emmanuel Adebayor scored a goal with a well-placed side-foot shot that ended up nestled in the bottom corner. That Adebayor goal triggered a chain reaction that would end up changing our focus and our mindset. The ball had come at Adebayor so fast and I had been so impressed that I was moved to mention it in my post-match press conference. On Monday morning, my manager pulled me aside and said, 'Yes, it was a good goal, but we never compliment Arsenal anymore. I'm sick of it. From now on, nobody compliments Arsenal.' He called a players' meeting to hammer home the same message.

From that moment we never said a nice word about Arsenal and a very curious thing happened. We became tougher to beat when we played them. We became steelier and more resolute, because we were no longer in the frame of mind that said, 'Oh, we'll probably get beaten today.'

The small adjustment in attitude by our manager had a profound effect on us as a squad. We altered the subconscious belief that had been dictating our playing standard. We would go on to become a team that had a much tougher belief system wired into it. After that, we regularly beat Arsenal and in time wondered what had ever been so great and wondrous about them.

Did you watch the European Championship final between France and Portugal?

It was a perfect example of how psychology is a key part of players' development.

In the previous weeks, it had been fascinating to watch the patience and diligence that the Portuguese players applied to their task. As the tournament progressed, there was a tendency to diagnose their failure to win any of their early matches within 90 minutes as an overreliance on Cristiano Ronaldo.

Undoubtedly, Ronaldo was the dominant figure in the squad – as he would be in any team he ever plays for. He has the skills to carry it off but in France he looked tired after a long season, and Portugal had no other comparable offensive threat in their ranks.

Such is Ronaldo's presence that when he went off early in the final he presented his teammates with the perfect excuse for losing. It was like Adebayor's goal against us years ago. Portugal, *if they had been us*, would have said, 'Well, here we go, the inevitable is about to happen.' Somewhere not too deep in his subconscious, each player would have started to think, 'Well, playing the host nation in a final with our greatest player sidelined is a scenario in which losing wouldn't be unexpected.' After the Paris bombings just months earlier, there was great deal of goodwill being channelled towards a French win. The role of honourable, sporting and surprising runners-up would be a good one to fill. People would say that Portugal had enjoyed a good tournament; they had done more than expected; the Ronaldo injury couldn't have been helped. The future was bright, blah blah blah ...

They never bent, though. They managed to control that subconscious train of thought. The longer the game went on, the more you could see that they intended to win. Ronaldo's injury wasn't an excuse to lose; it became an overwhelming incentive to win. In the final, the French never surfed on the passion of their home crowd. The whole occasion inhibited

THE SECRET PSYCHOLOGIST: VISUALISE EXECUTE REPEAT

Matt Taylor, the former Portsmouth, Bolton and West Ham set-piece specialist, had a very organised mind and understood that consistency of thinking gives you consistency of play. I helped him to create a list of four points that he would repeat to himself before every corner and free-kick he took.

Point one was to place the ball and visualise exactly what he wanted to happen. Point two was to step back, pause and tell himself to beat the first man. Point three was to commit to the plan in his mind. Point four would be to execute his technique 100 per cent – the trigger for that was to remind himself to plant his standing foot firmly, at which point the rest of Matty's technique naturally followed. Visualise, execute, repeat. That is the mantra that anybody can follow if they already know what it is they are looking to achieve.

them. The Portuguese did what they'd done in every game. They got better as it progressed. It wasn't beautiful but it was hugely impressive.

One way to build upon the subconscious – to control it without inhibiting it – is a process called visualisation. Bear this in mind the next time you watch Ronaldo's body language when he's taking a free-kick. His posture may look to you to be part of an image pegged to an inflated ego and a sizeable cheque from Nike. The reality is very different. At the moment Ronaldo places the ball on the floor, he is meditating. It is what psychologists call the power of positive thinking, or what is more commonly referred to in football circles as a 'visualisation technique'.

So watch Ronaldo the next time he is awarded a free-kick. You shouldn't have to wait too long. From the moment he has the ball in his hands he is visualising the outcome. Keep your eyes on him. He is in a cocoon. He goes into a pre-planned routine where he will never look at anything else. He doesn't talk to anybody and he doesn't even look at the referee as he waits for the whistle. Everything about the routine is a series of visualisation steps taught to him when he was young by a psychologist who started with a very simple question: What is it that you want to achieve, Cristiano?

In this case, the answer is obvious: Ronaldo wants to score. But you can't prepare to score a free-kick unless you consciously tell yourself that's what you're trying to do. It's not like scoring an ordinary goal, which can rely on subconscious thinking. This is a set piece and it must be executed with conscious thinking. So Ronaldo accesses his mental-clippings library of all the times he has scored from free-kicks. He runs through one or two in his brain. Slowly, so that his muscles can feel and remember the sensation. It's what is known as keeping your eyes on the prize.

The psychologist put in place a series of steps to help Ronaldo achieve his target.

1. Plant the ball.
2. Stand up and plant the right foot next to the ball to ensure the ground is solid.
3. Take one large step back while looking at the goal.
4. Take as many smaller steps back as dictated by the distance of the ball from the goal, also while looking at the goal.
5. Stand with legs apart and take a deep breath.
6. Focus on the goal and the exact piece of net that you want to hit.
7. With the image of the goal in your mind, look down at the ball and tell it that's where it's going to end up.
8. Start your run, focusing on your steps.
9. Direct all your energy into the ball on contact.
10. Follow through right to the end.

And roughly speaking those are the steps that help Ronaldo to deliver. His free-kicks routinely trouble goalkeepers. In these terms, Ronaldo is consciously aware of his actions.

Back in 1980, two sports psychologists, John Syer and Chris Connolly, began an association with Tottenham Hotspur

Football Club that would last five years. The initial reaction when news got out was hilarity and subtle mockery. One newspaper ran the headline, 'White Coats at White Hart Lane'.

One of the first things that Syer and Connolly introduced at Spurs all those years ago was this practice of visualising the situation, thinking it through meditatively and slowly and so often that when it began to unfold on the pitch you knew what to do without thinking.

Steve Archibald, a perennially miserable striker Spurs had at the time, once went to the sports psychologists and said that he'd lost confidence in his touch. He was asked to visualise the times when his touch had been sublime, when he was master of the ball without even having to think about it. How did he feel at those moments?

'Like the lord of the manor,' he said.

He was encouraged to keep thinking that he was lord of the manor.

The sports psychologists who went into Spurs in those early days would have faced a lot of resistance, but they had a supportive manager in Keith Burkinshaw and some players like Archibald who were willing to try anything. Take meditation/visualisation. When meditation first came into football clubs, it was a non-starter for most players. It was so far removed from what we were used to that I remember many players simply reading the paper while the instructor, eyes closed, sat in front of us for 15 minutes humming like a maniac.

We were footballers. We didn't want to tell anybody how we felt at any particular moment. Winning good. Losing bad.

That was about as complex as our emotions were allowed to get. Telling somebody in a suit that you felt like the lord of the manor? You could end up a laughing stock.

Many of my teammates didn't see the value of it because, back then, nobody could tell us how the technique related

THE SECRET PSYCHOLOGIST: SPEED OF MIND TRIGGERS SPEED OF BODY

I taught Stephen Warnock, the former Liverpool and Aston Villa left-back, a visualisation technique to help him become reactive and increase speed over the first two yards when defending against opposition players. Full-backs will always tell you that the most important part of one-on-one defending for them is the speed of their feet over the first two yards, particularly from a standing start, in order to stop wingers from making the by-line and getting a cross in.

When he had to get out of the blocks quickly, or turn and run to chase down an opposing attacking player, his cue would be to say to himself, 'I run on hot coals.' By imagining that he was running on hot coals he was able to accelerate and use the imagery to increase speed responsively. Not only was this a useful visualisation technique, but it also worked as a trigger. As soon as he had the cue, his muscles automatically responded to the prompt in his mind.

to football. Now they can. We understand our minds and bodies, and we can play tricks on them rather than the other way around.

Visualisation as a technique is at its most obvious in rugby, where it was arguably introduced into the mainstream by Jonny Wilkinson, the English fly-half and expert kicker. His routine provoked a collective raising of eyebrows when he first began doing it, but Wilkinson was deadly with the boot from all over the pitch and the rugby fraternity was forced to sit up and take notice. Today, every single fly-half of every level has his own routine when kicking the ball, his own form of meditation.

In a warm-up routine borrowed from Clive Woodward, England's rugby World Cup-winning manager, footballers are now engaging with their peripheral vision by having coaches drop a ball almost behind their head and reacting to catch it before it hits the floor. This is a routine used on strikers and central defenders, who are not always in the right position to see the whole picture. In the rugby version, players had to pass the ball to each other across the line without turning their head.

Football has learned a lot from rugby in terms of visualisation techniques. The big clubs on the continent now realise that they need to give the brain a stretch before a game and not just a player's leg muscles.

THE SECRET PSYCHOLOGIST INTERRUPTS

The best practice facility in the world is in our mind. We can slow down, speed up or zoom in and out on our technique and see the improvements we wish to make. Through visualisation and repetition of imagery, we can gain a better understanding of what success looks like.

Let's take a closer look at the performance technique of visualisation. Sometimes augmented by the use of hypnosis (yes, it can work), it is a tool that can and should be used by all those wishing to improve their performance.

The process of mentally practising your performance is useful to prepare for an upcoming competition, enhance the learning process, replay a past great outing or even to 'practise' effectively handling difficult performance situations. As a mental skill, visualisation is a good tool for you to add to your mental-toughness toolbox. The following principles and guidelines will help you learn to use your imagination to take your game to the next level, whether or not you do it through hypnosis.

- Mental rehearsal is the systematic recreation of a performance experience. It is not just 'seeing' in your mind's eye, but hearing, smelling and, most importantly, feeling what you would were you actually in that competitive situation. The effectiveness of visualisation lies in a player's ability to mentally create, in as much vivid detail as possible (seeing, hearing, feeling etc.), the performance.

- As with any skill, visualisation takes practice. Some players naturally 'see' things better in their mind's eye. Others don't see really well but can almost 'feel' as if they were actually performing. Still others have the ability to vividly play an experience in their head with all the critical detail, to the point where it almost appears real to them. Then there are players who try to do visualisation and all they 'see' is a blank or dark screen. Be persistent when you practise and keep at it. With daily repeated practice, you will improve your ability to 'see', 'feel' and 'hear'.

- Try to adopt an internal perspective. You can do mental rehearsal from two perspectives: internal or external. In an internal perspective, you see, hear and feel everything as if you were actually in the performance. In an external perspective, you see yourself performing from the outside, as if you were a coach watching yourself play. Some players use both perspectives simultaneously – Steve Warnock, Thomas Bjørn, Laura Robson, for example. That is, while they see themselves from the outside, they can actually feel what they'd feel if they were inside of the performance. Both perspectives are useful; however, learning to feel yourself inside the performance is always ideal.

- Begin every mental-rehearsal session with relaxation. Visualisation breaks down when the player is nervous or anxious. For your images to be as vivid and therefore as useful as possible, precede your practice with three or four minutes of relaxation. Similarly, be sure that your visualisation is done in an environment that's quiet and free from distractions.

- Have a specific goal for every visualisation session. That goal could be working on trying to get a better feel for a specific part of your performance. For example, let's say that you're a defender and your turns are weak. You can 'practise' the proper feel of a turn – attacking the ball, pushing off the target man, the first stride after the turn, the feeling of creating distance quickly between you and their front man, the first contact and control of the ball. Your goal could also be staying calm and relaxed just before or during the task. If this were the case, then you'd mentally practise experiencing yourself staying calm and composed when it counted the most.

- Use only peak-performance imagery leading up to an important event. Coping imagery involves experiencing yourself handling upsetting or problematic situations – perhaps you made a mistake and you want to practise mentally rebounding quickly and getting right back in the performance. However, a week before and then right up to that big event, you need to stop the coping imagery and only practise seeing yourself performing at your best.

- Make sure you stop using visualisation at the right time before you compete. Some players can successfully use mental rehearsal right up until they perform. Many others, however, have found that when they use visualisation the night before or closer to the competition, it generates anxiety and backfires, hurting not helping performance. The key is to figure out when is best for you as an individual athlete to stop using the skill before a competition. This is a trial-and-error proposition.

- Make your visualisation sessions short. Mental rehearsal is far more effective when it's done in short sessions (10 minutes or so) rather than longer ones. A good rule of thumb is more frequent, shorter practices.

- Focus on the process in your visualisation sessions, not just the performance outcome. The most effective mental practice involves 'practising' the proper technique and strategies. In your sessions, concentrate on repeating the correct technique, feel, timing etc. rather than just on the game's outcome. It's fine to imagine the outcome that you want, but that should be a minor part of your mental rehearsal.

I remember hearing the story of a US pilot who was held as a prisoner in the Korean War. As a nine-handicapper, he was obsessed with golf. In the four years of his captivity, he acted out playing his local golf course on almost a daily basis. He'd place the tee, assess the wind and distances, and play the ball. He would then decide where the ball had landed, find it and hit again. When he eventually returned to his hometown in Ohio, one of the first things he did after his recovery was play that favourite golf course. He played to handicap.

Experiments with basketball players at Chicago University have shown that practising with the ball, practising physically but without the ball, and rehearsing simply in the mind with no physical movement have yielded the same results in improved technique.

Visualisation is an important aid for players who are injured. I worked with Steven Reid, Roque Santa Cruz and James Perch when they were injured. I gave them techniques based upon visualisation, but also threw in a few others.

I asked them to watch the game from the bench, stands or TV and imagine that they were the manager. What decisions would they make? What would they be seeing and thinking? How would they win the game? I also asked them to watch the next game with a view to picking a man of the match. Who would it be and why? Or maybe to watch the game and choose a 'champagne moment', something brilliant that was maybe missed by the majority as it takes a special insight to see a flash of skill that usually goes unnoticed. I got them to concentrate on a unit they were not part of, and think what they would be doing if they were. So for Roque, if you were defending today, what would you be doing? Who would you be looking out for? Trying to stop? Wary of?

These techniques keep the injured player in the game. It stimulates them and gives them an opportunity to think differently and comprehend the game from a different perspective, increasing their knowledge and understanding. You can do the same with your local club side or even just watching a game on TV.

There is a saying, 'Never waste a good crisis' – and I think the injured player has the opportunity to come back stronger and better, and very much part of the team.

12. SOME HOME TRUTHS

What they don't teach you at St George's

So there you have it. Surprisingly all of the immense and complex problems of modern English football and, if you read carefully enough, English society have been solved by one former footballer with an interest in behavioural psychology.

Thank you, TSF, cries the grateful nation.

Alas, my work isn't yet done.

How do you, as one individual, make it through the jungle of football and end up as king? Because, let's face it, the difference in skill level in the Premier League between the best players and the most ordinary players is probably just a couple of percentage points. Further down the food chain, not much divides the winners from the also-rans of the lower leagues.

The difference lies in the way your brain works.

There are some things that nobody else will ever tell you. One of the most important things about rules is that being the exception to the rule, or just ignoring them, often puts you one step ahead of the herd.

FAKE IT TILL YOU MAKE IT, BABY

There are libraries filled with books defining what confidence is. And whole rooms within that library defining what sports confidence is. But when you decide to be a footballer, the FA doesn't arrange for everybody to be given the same amount of confidence. If you're lacking in the confidence arena, try what psychologists call 'impression management'. In other words – fake it.

Brian Clough was a genius. That doesn't mean he wasn't mad. As well as being the only British manager in history to win back-to-back European Cups (now the Champions League, kids), Clough liked to run his players through a waist-high bed of stinging nettles. His favourite time to do this was at the end of a pre-season running session in the heat of summer, when his players would have rolled down their socks, pulled up their shorts and taken off their training tops.

They were different times. If a manager asked a squad of modern players to do that, they'd pick him up, chuck him into the nearest nettle bed and never speak of him again.

My point (and, in case you were wondering, I do have a point) is to think about the impression you are giving off, regardless of whether or not it reflects how you really feel. I remember a pre-season tour in Austria, where a kayaking trip had been scheduled. Before we were due to leave, the manager called us into a room and told us that the area had just seen unseasonably high levels of rainfall. The river was dangerously swollen. Instructors had taken out a group of locals who were used to the river and knew it well. Two of them had drowned. I'll never forget it. He stood there in the centre of that room and said, 'All those who still want to

TSF PSYCHOLOGICAL TIPS: AVOIDING A YELLOW CARD

Here's a tip for when you want to avoid a yellow card. You know when you've fouled somebody and it's going to be a yellow card; you feign injury in an attempt to avoid the inevitable. When you're on the floor – don't move. Referees, like any member of the armed forces, are trained to go to the person who isn't moving before giving attention to anybody else. If you don't move and the referee comes over to you, then he's in a tough spot from an empathetic point of view. You bide your time, slowly come round, maybe allow yourself to be carried off, no yellow card. To give it the best possible chance of working you need to make the referee think that you have a head injury. They are absolutely terrified of showing no sympathy in the case of a potentially serious injury. They can see themselves on the front pages of the tabloids on Monday morning. It doesn't always work but I've seen it work enough times to make it worth having a go.

go, please move to the right. All those who don't want to go, move to the left.'

In the two seconds that we were given to weigh the positives of certain death against the negatives of looking like a coward, I deduced there was no way that a Premier League football club would endanger tens of millions of pounds of talent on a fucking kayaking trip. I was clever like that. I could rationalise the reality of the situation rather than taking a scenario at face value as most players do. In another walk of life, some big ugly corporation would have paid a lot of money for that trait – the civil service maybe? But no, I had to become a footballer. Stupid!

I thought about it and weighed it up: insurance, angry chairman, grieving fans. The Austria Kayak Disaster might not be up there with the Munich Air Disaster in the public imagination, but it wouldn't be a good move to be the manager who had sent us out on to those waters. So I moved into the 'yes' camp along with 75 per cent of the squad. The remaining 25 per cent were all foreign players, mostly Africans who couldn't swim.

Why did I do that? I realised that, in the absence of any kayaking, the manager was conducting a crude little experiment. It was the 'if you're not willing to die for me and the club and each other, then you're not willing to die on the pitch either' experiment.

There was no fucking way on earth that I was actually going to go kayaking, but if the manager wanted to see who his brave boys were, then I was willing to pretend all the way to the river bank. Clough's little nettle experiment had the same intention. OK, it wasn't a matter of life and death, but running through 100 feet of waist-high stinging nettles was enough in Clough's mind to separate the men from the boys. If you ran through nettles and pretended not to even notice the stings you were Clough's type of man.

Clough saw who his reliable robots were and who his likely deserters were. Our manager didn't sell any of the players who refused to go to a watery death, but those players never featured in the games that were our six-pointers.

In football, the impression formed of you by coaches is pretty instant and often disastrous. 'Ha! No first touch,' they announce when they've just noticed you because for the first time in the game you have miscontrolled the ball. Doesn't matter what you do after. Or the impression will be about your psychological make-up. We all make up our minds about people within seconds of meeting them.

No doubt your mum told you that you are a unique little snowflake and more beautiful than all the other little snowflakes. Coaches don't give a shit about the wonder of you. You are product. Sell yourself.

As a product you have physical, technical, mental, tactical and lifestyle components. Maybe you don't feel too confident, but act it out anyway. People around you will respond to your perceived assurance, and the sap who is marking you might feel intimidated. And then, in a strange roundabout way, that confidence you were pretending to have starts to take hold.

According to studies, there are four stages to this process:

1. Being aware of having the need and opportunity to self-present.
2. Figuring out what you want to achieve and how this will help.
3. Measuring your chances of pulling it off.
4. Working out what specific elements you want to see in this version of yourself.

You'd be surprised how many footballers are very different people away from the training ground or the pitch, away from football.

If you come late into the game, presenting yourself as others want to see you is a good survival technique. Always pretend to be up for kayaking in dangerous waters.

REMEMBER, IT'S A SMALL WORLD, REALLY SMALL. YOU COULD ACTUALLY DECORATE IT ON YOUR WEEK OFF

Our friend Stanley Milgram – who we met early on in this book when he was supervising the administration of fake electric shocks – also conducted research into the 'six degrees of separation' theory, which later became the Six Degrees of Kevin Bacon game, which amused people back when we all knew who Kevin Bacon was.

The point is that football is a very small world. If you act like a dick at one club, then the chances are that every other club will get to hear about it. And there are enough footballers with your ability out there who don't come with your baggage, so clubs might take a punt on you if they are desperate, but they'll keep shunting you. Ask Mario Balotelli.

The flipside of this is that if you consistently present yourself as a good leader and a good dressing-room influence, the small world of football takes note of this too.

By the way, the six degrees of separation theory was debunked and derided for years. (Debunking and deriding are favourite practices among behavioural psychologists.) But in 2008 Microsoft examined the patterns and characteristics from a data set of 30 billion conversations among 240 million people on their Messenger system. From the data, they constructed a communication graph with 180 million nodes and 1.3 billion undirected edges (whatever they are. The only time I have an undirected edge is when I drink too much) and they created the largest social network ever to be constructed and analysed.

The result?

'We investigate on a planetary-scale the oft-cited report that people are separated by "six degrees of separation" and find that the average path length among Messenger users is 6.6.'

Back of the net, Stanley old son!

TAKE ALL THE MARSHMALLOWS AS SOON AS THEY ARE ON THE TABLE …

Everybody knows about the Stanford marshmallow experiment. Well, most of you parents out there will do, I'm sure.

It is a series of studies about delayed gratification led by psychologist Walter Mischel.

The premise is that a child gets offered a choice between one small reward provided right now or two small rewards if they wait for a while – the rewards taking the form of marshmallows. The tester would place a marshmallow on the table in front of the child and explain that they could either eat the marshmallow now or, if they left it for 15 minutes, then they could have two marshmallows. The tester would then leave the room and not return until the 15 minutes were up. Mischel and his team then revisited the children later in life, and measured their success as adults against certain criteria, such as their career progression and financial situation. What they found was that the kids who had been able to wait longer and so secured the increased reward scored much more highly across this range of life measures. Those kids who'd gobbled the marshmallow down straight away were shown to be life's – how shall we say? – also-rans. And the experiment showed that for every minute waited over the allocated 15, the chances of the child being even more successful in life increased.

Very good.

But if you are a footballer, grab the fucking marshmallows as soon as you see them and cram them into your mouth.

Your agent may be confident he can secure a good deal for you, but he doesn't know for sure. Very often he is playing poker with a blindfold on. He may think he is holding three kings but his opponent might have four aces stashed. There

TSF PSYCHOLOGICAL TIPS: FLUSHING OUT A DEAL

Some football clubs like to wait until the last minute to conclude some of their transfers. Daniel Levy, the Tottenham chairman, is a notorious latecomer to the transfer market. There are certain footballers who perhaps aren't the number-one transfer target for a club and who have to wait for the targets above them to drop out one by one. But the players above them like to keep their own options open until the last minute, and that calls for a gentle nudge. My agent once put my name in the *Sun* transfer-rumours column in order to flush out a club that was on the fence.

This is done by claiming that another club has had an offer accepted for the player. It should never work in a million years but for some reason it does – it actually panics clubs into picking up the phone to the agent and setting the wheels in motion. Certainly that was the case for me, and I benefited further because the same rumour flushed out another club, which helped to drive up the wages on offer at the first club. Bonus. And it's still happening to this day with players up and down the leagues. The rumour columns that you read in the national newspapers generally have the interested club deliberately wrong, but the player is usually on the move.

is no real way of knowing. Hence the hopeful plea: 'Look, let's put our cards on the table.' That's where it comes from.

All contract negotiations are different. The fixed point pertains to how much the club wants to keep the player and how much the player wants to stay and sign. The variables beneath that are market forces – who else wants the player, how much money he can get elsewhere, whether he wants to play abroad or for a better team, or closer to home maybe. Perhaps his family are unhappy, or maybe the player is after a longer contract. Going into these negotiations, the chief executive will have an idea of all of that information before making his offer. The job of the agent, in the absence of any concrete interest elsewhere, is to bluff it.

I had a great agent. His philosophy of negotiation was to find out how many marshmallows a club had and to get them into my mouth as quickly as possible.

In any contract negotiation there is a pot of money. To keep it simple, let's say that the club has budgeted £5m for your services over the length of a five-year contract. That £1m a year can be sliced in a few different ways: there will be a basic wage and various bonuses. But the player may choose a signing-on fee of £1m spread over the five years, in which case the basic wage comes down. If he asks for £500,000 as a signing-on fee spread over 5 years, then the basic goes up.

A basic wage is obviously a staple, and so is a signing-on fee. But bonuses are more arbitrary figures. They are a bit of an afterthought, to be honest. They are the deferred gratification. Clubs love deferred gratification.

You would be amazed by the number of strikers I know who are beyond ecstatic at receiving a bonus of £20,000 a goal. In their heads they think, 'Hey, if I can get 25 goals this season I'll be laughing.'

As a Premier League striker at a club outside of the top six, you are generally expected to score a minimum of 10–15 goals a season; anything more is a very decent return, above and beyond. A bonus for the club. Actually, 14 or 15 goals would be good. But there are four to five strikers in each squad and these days only one of them gets to start regularly. The strikers on the bench are usually on big goal bonuses and very average wages – for a footballer, at least. Slowly, over the course of the season, it dawns on a few of them that they've been completely stitched up. They should have grabbed all those marshmallows.

When I was a player, my agent advised me to substitute as many bonuses as possible while driving up the basic wage and the signing-on fee. So if the deal was £20,000 a week plus a £5,000 win bonus, he'd ask for £30,000 a week and a £2,000 win bonus, with no clean-sheet bonus, assist bonus or goal bonus.

Remember this: if you leave at the club's request a couple of years into your contract, then you are legally entitled to all of the outstanding monies left on your contract. Usually at least £1m in the Premier League. The club, however, will negotiate by holding on to any outstanding bonuses, such as a loyalty bonus, money after 50 games played, signing-on fees etc. ... but the basic wage is set in stone.

That, Mr Trump, is the true art of the deal.

And it's worth noting that a curious thing would happen during my negotiations. We would agree the basic wage that my agent demanded and then the club would negotiate the bonuses back in anyway. They would pull *more* marshmallows out of their briefcase. Not because they wanted my basic wage to come down – that was now set – but because football clubs genuinely believe that bonuses incentivise certain players. If you are on a bonus, you will be hungrier.

Strikers, for instance, should look at their goal bonus in the following context: at some stage there will be an awful run of fixtures, something like Manchester City, Arsenal, Southampton and Manchester United, and it is not beyond the realms of possibility that a striker won't even have a shot in any of those four games, let alone score. Then, the next run of games, fixtures that should whet the appetite of a striker such as Swansea, Burnley, Crystal Palace and Watford, seems that much tougher. Suddenly, eight games have gone by without a goal.

Or ... You break your leg on the opening day of the season. No bonuses for you. You argue with the manager and get sent to the youth team. No bonuses for you. Think on this: Mrs TSF thinks that I must have been the highest-paid youth-team player in the Premier League when I had been banished to train with them for the best part of a season. But if I hadn't played my cards right, I would have been the worst-paid youth-team player in the Premier League too, with a terrible basic wage and no chance of bonuses. But I wasn't.

When I walked off the senior training pitch every morning at the manager's request, all those marshmallows came with me. Every fucking one of them.

Stick the bonuses up your arse. Stick the marshmallows in your mouth.

AND ALWAYS ASK FOR THE BIGGEST NUMBER OF MARSHMALLOWS YOU CAN THINK OF

The classic example that psychologists use when talking about something else besides football is this: You are buying some piece of music kit for your living room. You are in a shop ready to shell out 500 quid for this bit of kit when your mate says he saw the exact same bit of kit for £400 in a shop near where he lives. So you hop in the car, drive to where he lives and he's right – you've saved £100!

A little while later you are replacing your car. You are sick of the Porsche and want to get into the Range Rover set. Everybody at the club is driving these things and your sense of individuality tells you that you should have one too.

You are looking at a model with all the bells and whistles and it costs £125,000. Your mate is with you again. He tells you that he knows a geezer who has a garage and he can sell you the precise same car for £124,900. You'd be saving £100 again, but this time you don't get into your car and drive across town. Instead, you tell your mate to shut the fuck up and buy the car for £125,000.

Each scenario is identical in terms of finance – make a short drive and save £100. But you feel that the £100 you might have saved on the car is less than the £100 you might have saved on the music kit.

When it comes to money all things are relative, not absolute.

Also – and psychologists don't mention this – you'd feel like a dick walking out of the Range Rover showroom just because you can save £100 by going to somebody else. You're not that mean. The Range Rover purchase involves a degree of face-saving that the music kit doesn't.

Football clubs are just as irrational. The less you ask for, the more they'll haggle. The more that £100 means to you, the more they'll fight you for it. Be a Range Rover, not a small amp. Let the chairman get his jollies on by boasting to his friends about how much he is paying you.

All the marshmallows.

SCREW ZEN, YOU CAN PLAY WHEN YOU ARE ANGRY

To follow the path, look to the master, follow the master, walk with the master, see through the master, become the master ...

Blah blah.

Your motivations are supposed to be deep and intrinsic, a well inside your soul that you draw from when needed. You listen to the wise words of the manager, you visualise like the sports psychologist told you, you meditate, you centre yourself, you get into that 'zone' we hear so much about and understand so little of.

I remember the rugby league player Ben Flower getting sent off after two minutes of a Grand Final against St Helens for punching a guy twice when he was on the ground. The first punch had knocked the other player out.

Ben Flower isn't a monster. He just got on the wrong side of the hair trigger we sometimes feel in matches. He lives with the regret and people will throw it in his face for the rest of his career and beyond, but what he said in an interview after his long ban was over made sense.

'The rivalry with St Helens is there and playing them in the Grand Final was crazy. I knew it was going to be massive. So you were hyped up to the max – and you've got to be to play in these big games.'

It wasn't as if his two punches came out of context. The big hits were going in hard and vicious from the second the game started.

Nobody is saying that what Flower did was a good thing, but in football we tamper with people's emotions too. Jason Puncheon was left out of the FA Cup final against Manchester United, having started 30 Premier League games for Crystal Palace. In a pre-match interview, his manager Alan Pardew said, 'He's got a lot of anger in him, but that's OK, anger can be a good thing coming from the bench, as long as he channels it in the right way.' Pardew – as well as making sure that the world was aware a potential managerial masterstroke might unfold later in the day – was bang-on.

Apparently, Puncheon was so angered by his failure to make the starting 11 that he'd even sent a text to Danny Murphy, a BBC studio pundit on the day, which Murphy was asked to repeat to the viewers by anchor Gary Lineker.

Murphy tactfully removed the expletives – by which point there wasn't an awful lot left.

Pardew knew what he was doing, of course. At Wembley 26 years previously, in the 1990 FA Cup final, the striker, Ian Wright, had been left out of the starting 11 by his manager, Steve Coppell. When Wright eventually came on to the pitch, seething with rage, he scored two goals which almost won the cup for Palace.

He told Gary Lineker about that day.

'I thought I'd done enough to be involved,' said Wright, 'but I was on the bench and itching to get on. I'm looking at the clock wondering when I'm going to get a chance and it's ticking, 60 minutes, 65 minutes and finally on 70 minutes I get a chance. When you see me running on to the pitch I am so angry by that point that within three minutes I'd scored.'

Pardew played with Wright in that final, and knew the importance of having at least one player who is absolutely champing at the bit to be involved and angry at the injustice of not being out there from the start. In the 71st minute of the 2016 final, Jason Puncheon, with a face like thunder, came off the bench to replace Yohan Cabaye. Seven minutes later, he scored the game's opening goal.

There are little examples of anger at work in every single game that's played. There are some standout moments, too. If I managed Wayne Rooney, for instance, I'd be hoping for him to get a nasty kicking early on in every game. I'd be hoping that whoever did the kicking got off scot-free. Rooney is great when he's angry.

We all remember when he was livid at not winning a free-kick against Newcastle at Old Trafford. He raged at the referee for a moment after picking himself up off the turf. Then he volleyed the life out of a dropping ball from 25 yards. It ended up in the top corner.

He didn't calm himself, find his centre and execute that volley with serenity in his heart. It was a goal born of pure anger. This time the anger had been channelled in the right way.

Anger channelled in the wrong way? Well, Ben Flower. Or any one of the red cards Wayne Rooney has been shown when the perceived injustice at not getting a decision has manifested itself in the need to take revenge. Very often at the expense of an opposition player's legs.

Would you sedate him and calm him? Never. You keep him angry and hope for the best.

Anger is a powerful tool, but it has boundaries, as we've seen above. In the case of Rooney, anger manifested in the right way is a volley into the top corner. Manifested in the wrong way, it is a red card. In the short term, anger is fine because it stimulates motivation.

You can let your soul stand cool and composed before a million universes, or you can play like a freaking maniac.

Whatever gets you through the night.

ACTUALLY, REVENGE IS BEST SERVED HOT

I have always been a Spurs fan. We were playing Spurs one day and it was roasting hot. The ball went out for a throw and the ball boy jumped up to get it. Myself and Michael Dawson ran to the sideline. There was one bottle of juice. Powerade, I think. He reached it first and I stood next to him with my arm out, waiting for the last drops to be offered to me, which is normal. But Dawson drank it all. He didn't want all of the bottle; he drank it because we were standing right next to the Spurs fans and they all cheered because there was none left for me and I looked like a dick with my arm held out.

He didn't say anything. Just jogged back into position.

In football terms, Michael had just 'pied me off'. Fine. When he threw the empty bottle away, the whole east stand laughed at me. OK.

Michael's problem is that he's a 'nice boy'. 'Don't dish it out if you don't like what comes back' should be the inscription over his locker. He knows what he has coming and he starts to warn the referee. If he'd winked, raised his eyebrows or laughed out loud I could have tolerated it. But he didn't. He'd made me look like a cunt and jogged off like a prick.

And that's when I decided to end Michael Dawson's career.

It would be six months before I'd get the chance to play against him again. Too long.

I called players up and down the country. I called friends of friends. There are about two degrees of separation in football, remember. I called coaches. I even called a manager. I called anybody I could in order to find somebody who might cripple Michael Dawson for me.

Now, that isn't the done thing when you've been in academy and professional football since you were seven years old, but I missed those classes.

Despite offers of a bribe and a whole lot of begging, only two players I knew put in challenges on Dawson that struck me as ungentlemanly. Their heart wasn't in it and I couldn't blame them. 'He did what? Drank the last of a Powerade bottle? So ... then what did he do ...?' I carried the anger around with me for months afterwards, though. By the time we played Spurs again it had dissipated a bit. I tried to elbow him every chance I got, and very often I was successful, but by then my heart wasn't in it either.

I hope he knew why and how lucky he was. This does not make me a bad person.

TOGETHERNESS COMES IN MANY FORMS

The art of building a squad of players likely to win more games than they lose lies, of course, in talent.

Maybe.

I've played in teams that have swept all before them because they just had the right mix of ingredients.

For example, a little clique of players is fine when the team is winning. Nobody minds. It's a source of banter. Things work in reverse when the team is losing.

We have too many French players. They don't care enough.

Those two are cooking up a plan to escape to another club when this ship goes down.

They think they are better than the rest of us.

What are they fucking laughing about over there?

And so on.

As my dad used to say every Sunday when we had our meat dish for the week, 'You don't know how lucky you are.' I'm pretty sure he meant that we didn't know how 'circumstantial' our lives were. He didn't think I knew the meaning of that word at that age.

Anyway, you can have all the talent in the world in a squad but whether you have the right people is usually down to luck or circumstance.

Enjoy it while it lasts.

CONCENTRATION IS ... WELL, I'M GLAD YOU ASKED ME THAT, GARY

When it came to concentration I was a repeat offender. My mind wandered everywhere.

I have been playing against the top sides and been so bored that I've actually interviewed myself on the pitch. Sometimes, I've interviewed myself in the last five minutes of a game when we're 3–0 down: the media ask, 'So what went wrong today?' and I say, 'Well, I think it was a number of issues ...' And I explain them and finish on a downbeat little joke that shows I hate losing but I'm never a dick about it.

More fun is when we are 3–0 up and the first question is, 'So, you were magnificent today – just how far can you and this group of players go?'

'Listen, I get the plaudits today but really I'm only as good as the lads around me. We've got a real sense of togetherness in the squad; these lads would run through walls for each other and I just feel privileged to be a part of it.'

What a modest, level-headed guy.

(You should be able to spot the players interviewing themselves on the pitch. They're the ones who've gone misty-eyed and distant when the game has hit a lull.)

Or sometimes, when the ball goes dead, you'll catch a glimpse of a shock of blonde hair in the crowd and make eye contact with a beautiful woman. Just for a moment you're not focused on football anymore. You have to force yourself back.

Concentration for 90-plus minutes isn't natural.

REALLY, IT'S OK IF DEEP DOWN YOU ARE VERY SHALLOW

Of course you love the game. Always have. Man and boy. You love the club. Always will.

You get paid well but it's all such an honour that you'd do it for free; you'd do it for the love of it. You'll play parks football from when you retire until your legs are useless stumps. Then you'll go in goal.

Not really. Psychologists love investigating these things. They've discovered that what you really crave is an audience. Cyclists ride with greater intensity when there is a crowd watching. Weightlifters lift significantly more heavy stuff when they have an audience. Football teams score more goals. When we do something that we are confident about and well rehearsed in, we do it better if there are people watching us.

If a tree falls in the forest and there is nobody there to see it, does it make a sound? Screw that. What if you score a 40-yard screamer in one of those games that gets played behind closed doors as punishment for crowd trouble. Does it even count? Can it be goal of the season? Do you feel like a twat running in the direction of an empty terrace and sliding on your knees towards the concrete when you get there?

Teams play better in front of full houses than they do in front of half-empty stands. They are better at home partially because all the people watching them think that they are great. The presence of other people increases our drive.

We want money and approval. We're the same as everybody else, really.

THE GAFFER IS HUMAN, BE PATIENT

A psychologist called Tom Gilovich once conducted a famous study to examine what is known as the 'hot hand' phenomenon. According to the theory, when a basketball player has two free throws after a foul his chances of landing the second are influenced by his success in landing the first. If he scores first time round, he's more likely to score again with the second. Gilovich found that each throw had an independent probability of success. There was no 'hot hand'.

The experiment has been disputed and argued over in academic circles ever since, but the reaction of sports coaches was summed up by the celebrated Boston Celtics coach, Red Auerbach, when he was asked about the study.

'So he made a study ... I couldn't care less.'

Coaches and managers are interested in all the stuff that confirms what they think they already know. You know better? They couldn't care less.

Social psychologist Ziva Kunda once performed an experiment in which she brought participants into a room and told them they were about to play a game. Before they started, they would watch two other people play the game. The game being watched was a fake, and one of the players involved appeared to be far superior to the other.

Kunda told half of the volunteers that this virtuoso player would be their teammate. She told the other half that the virtuoso would be their opponent. The participants who lined up to play alongside this apparently great player praised his skills hugely. Those who lined up to play against him dismissed his skills and decided he was just lucky.

Managers do this all the time. It's motivated reasoning, apparently. We emphasise whatever it suits us to emphasise.

Just roll with it.

PUNDITS ARE RODENTS BUT ...

In his book, *Expert Political Judgment*, the psychologist Philip Tetlock describes an experiment that he saw years ago at Yale.

A rat was placed into a T-shaped maze. Food was positioned at either the right or the left tip of the T shape in a random sequence. Over the long run, the food was on the left side 60 per cent of the time and on the right 40 per cent of the time. The students and the rat all started out with the same level of knowledge. That is, none were clued in to where the food would be 60 per cent of the time or 40 per cent of the time.

The students were asked to predict which side of the T the food would appear in each time. Now, the rat eventually figured out that the food was on the left side more often than the right, and it therefore nearly always went to the left. Its score for the test was around the 60 per cent mark. The students screwed up by looking for patterns of left–right placement. On average, the students got it right about 52 per cent of the time.

The conclusion was that the rat, never having studied at Yale or appeared on *Match of the Day*, had no reputation to begin with. The rat didn't find it embarrassing to be wrong 40 per cent of the time. Yale students, who have expensively acquired reputations, couldn't tolerate that percentage rate of failure and looked for hidden sequences. They ended up being wrong almost half the time.

The core of Tetlock's book is a study he made over the course of 20 years. He recruited 284 people who made a living from 'commenting or offering advice on political and economic trends' and he asked them, as experts, to assess the probability of certain political and world events. Tetlock assessed the method they employed to make their judgements, their reactions when their predictions were wrong, their evaluation of information not in agreement with their prediction, and their assessment of rival theories and predictions.

To make things clearer from a statistical point of view, he framed his forecasting questions in terms of 'three possible futures'. The experts were asked to cut the waffle and to rate the probability of three alternative outcomes: the persistence of the status quo, more of something (political freedom, economic growth) or less of something (repression, recession).

He measured the answers of the experts on two scales: how good they were at guessing probabilities, and how accurate they were at predicting specific outcomes.

The results, as the *New Yorker* reported, were alarming: 'Human beings who spend their lives studying the state of the world ... are poorer forecasters than dart-throwing monkeys, who would have distributed their picks evenly over the three choices.'

Unless you're putting money on it, nothing is at stake in the prediction business except reputation. The reputation that football journalists have among footballers is – what's the word now? – low. Very, very low. Their predictions are, of course, no better than yours. They're rarely held accountable if they are wrong and they rarely ever refer to that wrongness again except in epochal events like Leicester winning the Premier League, in which case they note that even they didn't see that coming. Nobody saw it coming, and if nobody saw it coming, how could I, a mere expert in the field, see it coming?

And do they learn? Do they revise their beliefs on a constant basis, seeing as they are almost constantly wrong? Rats do. Pundits don't. Notice how nobody wants to say that Leicester will get relegated this season? Not publicly anyway. I don't think they will. But they might. And nobody wants to say that Leicester will win the league again. I don't think they will. But they might.

When it comes to analysis, pundits are disaster areas. Full of confirmation bias and motivated reasoning or, in layman's terms, crap. They are classic poster boys for what is called the narrative fallacy. In other words, they have a limited ability to look at sequences of facts without forcing an explanation on to them.

When Chelsea win a game, the boys back in the *Match of the Day* studio pick out maybe 90 seconds' worth of highlights. Or they have 90 seconds of highlights picked out for them. They use the highlights to point to good shots, clever passing, an intelligent run off the ball, tracking back, defenders covering round. Whatever. Thus they create the illusion that they understand exactly why Chelsea won.

All there is to being a TV expert is hindsight and post hoc explanations. The true test of any pundit's explanation of a football game is whether what they are pointing to would have made the event predictable in advance. And whether they ever pointed that out in advance.

Predicting things is great fun. Only professional pundits take it seriously, though.

For any young player reading this, take it from me, if you want to win at punditry (which I assume is probably the furthest thing from your mind right now), then see it not as a vocation but as an opportunity.

Never say anything controversial or new.

Someday it will pay off.

THE SECRET PSYCHOLOGIST INTERRUPTS

A lot to digest here. Let me cherry-pick a few topics.

THE MARSHMALLOW TEST ...

I smiled when I got to the bit about marshmallows and contracts.

Contracts are fascinating because of the role they play in attracting, retaining and allowing the talent to perform. TSF wanted me to write something about Derren Brown and the type of influence and persuasion techniques that can be applied psychologically to such a situation.

TSF disappoints me. I know that he is a man of integrity and would not use such manipulation to gain the upper hand. However, I would. You have to remember that magicians are guardians of empty treasure chests. What is presented for entertainment is not all that has taken place. This is not to say that stooges and camera tricks are deployed with psychological magic; in fact, the duplicity and psychological subtleties are still outstanding, but can the same techniques really be used in negotiation? I'm not sure.

If you read self-help books, you may notice there has been a radical shift in the way in which they present their content.

The self-help books from the 17th and 18th centuries used the language of 'character ethic', old-fashioned words like endeavour, servitude, loyalty (you could argue that the Bible was a self-help book pre-dating these works), and certainly for 350 years you would have found that these solid character-ethic words made up the bulk of the thoughts. But in the last 50 years there's been a big change. The majority of the thoughts and words have been about personality ethic. It's all about matching and rapport. How to shake hands correctly and look people in the eye when you're talking. A slap on the back and laughing at the right jokes and you'll go far ... *How to Win Friends and Influence People* being one of the first of these books.

Whether it's contract negotiation, managing your career or just being a bloody good team member, the way forward is character ethic.

Not only does it give us a North Star and moral compass to make the right decisions, but it also allows us to communicate them and have them understood. I also find that people with strong character ethic tend to be more motivated. They have an intrinsic motivation to express their values. This may not just be on the pitch, but in the way they conduct themselves and involve themselves with other things outside of football.

I would advise any player involved in contract discussions: negotiate with your purpose in mind. Too quickly, a player's eyes will light up at the prospect of a lucrative deal that means the cash will soon be rolling in and the trappings that were once out of reach are now firmly in range of his credit card. He agrees to the move and frantically signs away. He then travels to the other end of the country to play in a team that is failing or not conducive to maximising his talent. His friends and family are now 400 miles away and his evenings are spent with a Pot Noodle. True story.

How many careers must have been ruined by the smell of an extra few quid?

CONCENTRATION IS ...

TSF used to interview himself on the pitch late in matches. He's not the first or the last.

It is a truism that players who perform the best don't have to be the most technically gifted. They have to make the most of their talent, by choosing to use their skills to their utmost. Good-quality decision-making is essential.

Flawless games rely on a series of good decisions, as already discussed. To make a series of rapid and correct decisions, we need to be able to maintain the right levels of concentration. But here's the thing: we have a bottlenecked brain; if the brain is trying to process too much information at the same time, it ends up unable to process any of it at all.

Being able to focus your mind and keep your attention directed is really the foundation of every kind of mental

THE SECRET PSYCHOLOGIST: EMBRACE YOUR SHORTCOMINGS AND IMPROVE YOUR GAME

Sir Alex Ferguson told Phil Jones, the Manchester United defender, that he needed to improve the speed of his feet when opposing strikers were running at him. After studying Phil's performances over a number of weeks, I realised that it was less about the speed of his feet and more about the speed of his decision-making. I devised a very simple training-ground technique to improve the speed of his mind and therefore his decision-making. We would take a bag of balls and tell Phil to jog away from a coach who would at any point shout 'turn'. Phil would have to make a series of lightning-quick decisions, including which way to turn, how to deal with the ball that would then be thrown at him and which position his body needed to be in to best execute either the control of the ball and the pass out, or the clearance.

This overloading of the brain and forcing it to make a series of rapid decisions means that it doesn't have any room for negative thoughts and only has the capacity to ask questions relating to the situation. For example, a high ball dropping out of the sky means that a defender has time to fill his mind with negative thoughts about what he is going to do with it. The initial decision to perhaps head the ball or control it is then followed in the time that the ball takes to come to him with thoughts such as, 'I hope I don't mess this up', 'What will happen if I mess this up?' and so on until, inevitably, the player's concentration is distracted and the mistake happens.

Today, Jones is a much more rounded player and his speed of thought is razor-sharp. But he isn't pulling any sleight of hand and anybody, at any level, can learn these techniques and improve their game.

training. That's why it is so important to practise. I have sat in front of some of the best sportspeople in the world and they have asked me for techniques to enable improvement. Some of those people have come back a week later and said that they have tried it and it hasn't worked. This is the equivalent of hitting the gym for half an hour, going home, looking in the mirror and saying, 'That was shit, it's done nothing.' All mental techniques, just as with the gym, are about regularity and progress through iteration and feedback. Developing concentration is similar to developing physical strength – with patient, persistent practice the techniques I outline below will increase the strength and duration of your attention. You have to practise concentration techniques to improve concentration. Unfortunately it takes concentration to do so – see the paradox?

An improved level of concentration won't just help with your 90 minutes of football; it will enhance your ability to stay focused, 'on target', and to find a dynamic balance of flow and flexibility in your daily life. Here's an exercise you can do virtually any time to improve your concentration and your focused attention.

Notice a noise. It might be the TV or someone chatting next to you in a café or bar. Now focus on a fingernail. Look at your fingernail in detail. Take in the subtle colours and striations. Take note of the shape and structure. When you first do this, you'll have a 50:50 battle between the two stimuli. Just keep staring at the nail and try to lose yourself in the detail. If you can drown out some of the noise with your concentration, you're winning the attention battle. If you can manage to direct about 70 per cent of your attention and energy towards the nail and not the sound, then you're doing great. Just by doing this for two minutes, you'll be surprised how good you get at it.

Here are the five most important points to keep in mind as you develop your concentration. Use this list as a guide for successfully integrating the focused mind state into your daily life:

1. Emphasise quality, not quantity, of training time. Take breaks while your concentration is still good. This will leave you looking forward to continuing.
2. Practise regularly. Your mind is like your body: by working out several times a day for short periods you'll see better results than if you practised just once a month.
3. Initially, practise focusing your attention on objects or activities that you find beautiful or interesting. You can then build the power to transfer your attention to things that are less immediately appealing.
4. Be mindful throughout the day by directing focused attention towards your ordinary activities. Then, when you choose to really zoom in and focus on something, your mind will already be calm, collected and prepared to produce optimal results.
5. Finally, and perhaps most importantly, remember to smile and enjoy your 'concentration fitness' training. Build your power of concentration while doing the things you love to do. Enjoying your practice is an essential ingredient that will enhance your abilities and speed your progress.

Practising concentration techniques requires a dynamic balancing of many qualities of mind. On the one hand, it's like a bulldog sinking its teeth into an object and tenaciously holding on – yet it's also a fact that, with too much pressure, the mind will tire and soon lose its grip.

Surprisingly, some of the most effective concentration techniques are very basic. The simplest and most direct method for developing mental stability and concentration skills is to focus on your own breath. How often do we take note of the rhythms of our own bodies? Just focusing on how we're breathing enables us to become one with ourselves and connect in a more mindful way with our physicality.

As optimum concentration is like holding a delicate bird or butterfly in your palm, mimicking this physically isn't a bad way of practising. Place a small feather in your hand – the sort you can pull from a pillow. Hold it still for a minute; try not to see any movement, and concentrate on the stillness of the moment. Do this for as long as you like, and look for incremental improvements over time. You may not gain the Zen-like powers of a ninja, but it's a great way to learn how to create a still, consistent way of thinking.

The complex relationship between stress and concentration can be helped by some basic relaxation strategies that will help you maximise your concentration by releasing stress. One great way to enhance your powers of concentration is to regularly practise meditation.

If you can't be arsed with meditation – although I whole-heartedly recommend it for empowering the mind – just getting some proper sleep helps! There is a direct correlation between sleep and concentration levels. It is important for us to recognise the optimum levels of sleep and rest needed to mentally recharge and be able to attack each day refreshed and invigorated.

SCREW ZEN ...

Finally, the question of anger and also TSF's lukewarm vendetta against Michael Dawson.

Most people don't realise that anger is a secondary emotion usually experienced in response to a primary emotion such as hurt, frustration, fear – or seeing a bottle of juice finished off by Michael Dawson. Anger can be an almost automatic response to any kind of pain. It is the emotion most of us feel shortly after we have been aggrieved in some way, such as being left out of the starting line-up or being on the wrong end of a poor decision by the ref.

It is true that anger is a very useful emotion to feel in situations where you need to be confrontational, assertive or aggressive. However, some believe that anger is a wasted emotion, and there have been many studies to find out whether or not feeling anger could actually be beneficial to the individual, and whether or not their willingness to feel anger is related to emotional intelligence, or EQ. Emotional intelligence relates to an individual's ability to understand, reason and use emotions and emotional knowledge to better their thoughts and actions. It is argued that the greater the emotional intelligence, the greater the person's overall mental health and wellbeing. People with a high EQ were found to be able to take their anger and channel it into performance.

I often refer people to the FranklinCovey equation of E + R = O. That is, the event plus the reaction equals the outcome. The events are the incidents and accidents that push and pull us in different directions on a daily basis. The reaction is how we choose to do deal with them. I call it ResponseAbility: our ability to respond to a situation in a way that makes the most of the circumstance (E), no matter what it is. The outcome is the opportunity derived from the two being put together.

When I explain that our true power lies in the reaction (R) bit, people think I am talking about calmness when bad things happen. I am not. Maybe anger is the correct response to drive the best outcome.

There was talk at one stage of me doing some work with Wayne Rooney. I never did. One of the points on the brief was about reaction to events. The only thing I'll say is that if you try to curb the 'anger' or aggression in some players that may occasionally lose you a game, will the player then win you fewer games because he no longer has that trait as the positive force it could be? For some players, aggression is their equivalent of Samson's hair.

I have worked with many players and teams who have actually weakened a strength by trying to strengthen a weakness. It's ludicrous.

13. TIME ADDED ON

I grew up in a happy, unsuspecting time before Gary Neville had been invented.

We had no clue as to what lay ahead.

When we were kids, we didn't have pundits with giant screens and incredibly big arrows pointed at the heads of players who were just about to do something pivotal in a game. All we had were scraps of highlights. Occasionally, there would be the odd live game, where it was up to us to figure out what was happening and who was doing what.

Our street had about 20 kids (an early EU regulation – 21 per street was the maximum) and we were all football mad. Very often we'd cram together into a living room and watch the highlights while generously sharing our expert opinions.

'Barnes isn't past it,' somebody would say, 'it's because Mølby won't move out of the centre circle and Rush won't drop deep to link it.'

Gold dust.

Having to work out whether Barnes, Rush or Mølby was the problem was one of the joys of being a football geek.

After the highlights, we'd all pile 'down the back' and try to work out what was going wrong, or right, by playing it out ourselves. Imagine that, a kid actually going through all the scenarios of an attack and trying to work out which player was at fault. It was a beautiful learning curve. I loved it and I miss it badly.

I learned so much without even trying and I felt completely at home. Picking apart the minds and movements of top-flight footballers felt easy for me. It was second nature, something I was born to do, like I could do it in my sleep. It still feels like that.

We never really dreamed there'd come a time when those opinions would be spoon-fed to people sitting in front of their TVs. When there'd be no space for making up your own mind, no corner to be argued with your mates, no position that you had to justify by backing it up with actual knowledge.

Today, people ask me how they can watch football in the same way as a player or a manager or a coach might see it. And the answer is that all the information is in front of you. The game is going on in front of your eyes, just as it is going on in front of ours: the same players, same stadium, same game unfolding, same everything. The difference lies in the interpretation of what you are watching and how you *choose* to process the same information that everyone has. That's the big secret. Process the information and apply it in the way that you see fit. What marks out great managers and players who know what they're talking about is the way they perceive and apply information.

Fans might see a great piece of skill, and we might see a missed opportunity to develop a move. A fan might see what appears to be a great sliding tackle; we might see a player who had a chance to pinch the ball without going to ground before launching a counterattack against an exposed back four. You might boo him because you thought he ducked out of a 50:50; we would applaud him even if he didn't manage to pinch the ball. His decision was right because it represented a bigger picture that you might not be able to see. But all the information is in front of both of us.

Eventually, those kids I once dissected the game with grew up and did exactly what was expected of them. I didn't do what was expected of me. And I have asked myself the question many times: why is it that I, TSF, the handsome runt of that litter of 20 street kids, the kid who was naive in so many ways, never had any doubt that I would play in the Premier League against the best players and teams in the world?

I came up with some sort of an answer recently. It accounts for a lot of what has happened in my life and in my football career. I realise now that the little kid in the park, practising every single hour of the day, did so because he wanted it just that little bit more than anybody else and he was convinced that he was good at it.

At a time in life when every person who was in a position of authority was telling me to concentrate on school and to be sure to get a shitty part-time job to earn £10 a week, I refused. I wouldn't listen. I followed my own instinct and it served me well.

Since I first became aware of football as a little kid and for the majority of my life thereafter, I spent every waking hour trying to improve my chances of playing in the Premier League; every day was an argument, a discussion, a practice session, a video or a live match. I had my eyes firmly fixed on becoming a footballer and getting to the top.

I was focused on getting to the Premier League and I had the whole plan mapped out for how to do it. I had trained my brain and my body towards achieving that goal. And I believe, very firmly, that if you're desperate enough for something – I mean really desperate, to the point where it's all you can do not to think about it every single day, where it hurts you every day that goes past and you don't have it yet – then you will get it.

Your mind finds a way. It makes choices based on the net result; it is trained and driven, and, in its quest to deliver your body to the right destination, it fires up every emotion needed at the correct times, without you even realising it. And one day my brain and my body found their way to the Premier League. I made it. It was the culmination of my life's ambition, and a massive and very enjoyable slap to the head of anybody who had said I couldn't do it. Every day since then has been a gradual decline in my ambition, my hopes, my career and my life.

I had no plan for what to do once I arrived in the Premier League. And that was my biggest problem.

I had never given it a single thought. Getting to the Premier League was the sole aim in my life, not playing in it. When I began playing well in the Premier League, it felt empty. I didn't know where I was going or what it was all for; there was no journey to go on anymore, let alone a destination to arrive at. It felt, well, pointless, if you want the truth of it. When the media and my own manager first started touting me for England, I was mystified. I didn't want to do that. I'd never considered that I might play for England; it wasn't part of my plan, it was never a consideration at any point in my road map. I even did an interview that was subsequently pulled by the club's PR department, in which I stated that 'if England select me, then the lack of talent in this country must be more serious than we thought'. No player would ever say that today. But I did back then. I wanted to make a point. And I look at the England squad now and think, 'I'm glad I made that point, shame nobody listened.'

A part of me died the day I reached the Premier League, there is absolutely no doubt about that. My life's ambition, as it turned out, had been flawed from the very start, and that has played on my mind ever since. And I guess that's what I'm driving at. I'm sorry to come across as morbid, but it's an emotion that I've never been able to shift since the day I won promotion to the Premier League as a young man. It's an emotion that strikes at the very heart of an illness that we now call depression. It is the little voice in my head telling me that it's all a big nothing and that, one day, we'll all be dead anyway. It's important always to have a goal ahead of you, because otherwise what's the point?

I look at the span of my football career and it all happened, every moment, while my friend Lee Stephenson was in prison, dealing with one moment of madness. That should be perspective enough, shouldn't it? I know the price I paid for a flawed plan was pretty low in comparison. But regrets are regrets ...

Alan Bennett once said that he had lived his whole life with a voice in his head constantly telling him that the best was over. I'd trade the voice in Alan Bennett's head for the voice in mine.

My voice doesn't tell me that the best is over. It tells me that *everything* is over.

But the truth of the matter is that you reach a point in your career where you begin winding down. You become a little less enthusiastic. No manager says anything that you haven't heard before. Your career is behind you and not in front of you, so you become a little less keen to please.

I struggled with that. I can honestly say, with my hand on my heart, that I gave everything to get to the Premier League and everything once I was there; for me, the problem started when I came back down again. Some players enjoy that part of their career, but I was at home one night and my parents were round for dinner when I had what can only be described as some sort of panic attack.

It wasn't because I didn't play football in the Premier League anymore, although that was the root cause; it was because it suddenly hit me that the best was over. I had a very clear arc in my life for the first time. I had gone up the ladder, stayed at the top and was now coming back down. Failure? I wasn't sure. But I certainly felt that there was nothing left to shoot for.

When I began to fall back down the leagues, my enthusiasm for playing football drained out of me. The reality was shit. You always fear that you are running out of time. Too old to be a prodigy. Too old to be a good investment for a big club. Too old to improve significantly. Too old ever to make yourself into the global great you dreamed of being. Too old to play in a World Cup. Too old for another contract at this level.

You will never be as fit or as young, ever again.

Trust me. It's a body blow when the brain dumps all that shit on you at once. I felt shock, anger, uselessness and a need to see myself as an abject failure. Lots of players enjoy the autumn days of their career. I didn't. It was crushing to live through the reality of no longer being good enough.

I can remember a bitter old Glaswegian player once saying to me, 'Do yourself a favour, if you ever end up back at a club like this when you're older, just retire.' I was only a kid – well, 22 actually, but I had boyish charm – and I don't remember listening too intently. He stunk of booze every morning and he hated all life forms. The warning he was transmitting to me was not the one he intended to give.

I am retired now. The adventure is all over and done with. I read something a while ago about a behavioural experiment that was conducted in an old folks' home. Half the old folks were given jobs to do that involved them making decisions.

The decision might be when to play bingo, but the responsibility for the decisions was theirs. The others had nothing to worry about. They just had to sit and talk about old times and remember when there was no Gary Neville.

The result was unsurprising, really. The old people with things to do and decisions to make fared better health-wise and generally lived longer.

I knew how the non-decision-making group felt the day I retired. You have no place to go. No series of small decisions to make (what to do with the rest of my life? That's a big decision not a small one, and has to be deferred as long as there is something good on television). You aren't a footballer. You are an ex-footballer. They're cheering somebody else and some days it hurts.

There's an old story about Marilyn Monroe coming home to her then husband, the former baseball great Joe DiMaggio. Marilyn had been doing one of those tours among the troops, cheering up US soldiers in Korea or somewhere by making them feel they could die happy now that Marilyn Monroe had waved at them.

'How did it go?' asked DiMaggio.

'Oh, Joe, it was unbelievable. You have never heard such cheering.'

'Well, I have actually,' muttered Joe, who went to the kitchen to make himself a stiff drink.

Every retired player knows how DiMaggio felt.

At least the world will remember your moments of glory, though, right? Wrong.

In 1872 England played Scotland in the first official fixture of what would become arguably the fiercest rivalry in world football. Over a century later, in 1983, both nations walked out at Wembley locked on 39 wins apiece and 22 draws – it was a huge game. The captain of England that day was also the captain of the English FA Cup holders. The captain of Scotland that day also happened to be the captain of the reigning league champions and one of the most decorated club captains in english football. Some questions:

- Who were those captains?
- What domestic teams did they captain?
- What was the score in that game?
- What is the current swing of victories between England and Scotland?
- Where are those captains now?

One thing is for sure: all those lads in 1983 thought that they were the dog's bollocks. Football was big and they were big in football. And there were few games that were bigger anywhere in the world.

If I hadn't Googled it, I'd have had no idea about the answers to those questions. And I pride myself on knowing most of what is happening within our game in this country. The point is that, if it isn't your team, would you know? Would you care? Is football actually important? Or is football only important when your team wins something, and even then only for a short while? How much time is allowed to go by before the legends in the squad photo become a squad that fans have no affinity with, even though they played for their club. *Does football really matter?*

In 1975, England beat Scotland 5–1 at Wembley in a Home Nations match. Uh, excuse me, but what is a Home Nations match? Just accept that this was deemed to be an historic and unforgettable moment. Can you name any of the goalscorers? I mean, 5–1, that's a big score against the old enemy, isn't it? Surely worth remembering when the two play one another in the future and the BBC are trawling through the archives. 5–1. I couldn't name you a single goalscorer. Not one. Did you know that Don Revie managed England that day?

It's not just football. It's life. Every behavioural study I have quoted in this book came out to fanfare when it was published. Then, one by one, each of them got pissed on and debunked and argued into oblivion by the next generation of graduates.

You just have to try to remember that things wouldn't be as they are today if you hadn't done your little bit in the past. That's the key. That at least stops me worrying at night that I've wasted my life. Maybe it did mean something, even if it isn't so obvious now.

And it certainly felt like it meant something at the time. Having that drive to reach the Premier League, that sense of purpose, is a kind of happiness. It's important to have goals like this. But beware what your goals are.

You can spend your whole life trying to win at a succession of things that you feel are important to your wellbeing.

If you win, then you'll be able to buy that car or that watch or that house you want. And then you'll be happy and you'll have everything that you ever desired. Then one day it happens and you buy the watch and the car and the house. And you are happy. Or at least happier. For about a month.

But eventually the brain kicks in – 'we need more'. We still don't have that boat we've always wanted, or that bolthole in Ibiza that we always promised we'd get once we'd 'really won something serious'. And it never ends. The desperate pursuit of never-lasting happiness.

A great psychologist who lives not too far from here once told me about a recurring dream he had a few years ago when his father was dying. He would walk into a big, empty white room and see his father standing in the middle of it. The psychologist held in his hands a box and every night he would walk with it towards his father and open it in front of him.

The first night, the box was filled with jewels. There were rubies, sapphires and diamonds as big as fists. But his father looked disappointed. The next night, the psychologist entered the room again and this time opened the box to reveal bundles and bundles of cash, more money than anyone could ever spend. But his father again appeared disappointed. The next night, the box was filled with gold bars, but once more his father seemed disappointed. And so it went on. Until one night, exasperated, the psychologist entered the room and walked towards his father before opening the box. It was empty. A smile broke out across his father's face and then he vanished. The psychologist never had the dream again.

Psychology shouldn't really be confused with philosophy, another of my favourite subjects. Nevertheless, the two do sometimes collide when we wonder what life is all about. And it's not about money. It's good to have a goal to aim for, but be wary of making your goals physical or materialistic gains, because they will never be enough and they will never bring you lasting happiness.

I noticed it when I walked into a club that I used to play for. The ludicrous nature of celebrity. As an ex-player, I had been invited to a game. I'm not a fan of this sort of thing, to be honest. But along I went. As I walked in I found myself confronted with myself. There was a huge poster of me celebrating a goal I scored once upon a time against some other bunch of losers. I still have some standing at the club and that has become a famous picture.

Weird. As I gazed up at it, I felt at ease with the first half of my life's work. The moment led me to a conclusion.

I signed a lot of autographs that day and talked to a lot of people. I could see fathers telling their children, who never even saw me play, who I was and what I'd done for their club. Then they'd push the poor kid towards me to get an autograph. It was fun and it was exhausting.

That night I came back to the house and slunk into the bath. It's not about money, or jewels or gold bars; it's about happiness. It's about being comfortable with who you have become and what you represent. That empty box my psychologist friend showed to his father represented contentedness for both men. That blown-up picture of me scoring a goal?

TSF PSYCHOLOGICAL TIPS: EGO MANIFESTS ITSELF IN VERY UGLY WAYS

Pet hate. Sometimes, when players achieve a promotion or win a trophy they feel the need to tell the world who they are. Usually these players are subs, but occasionally they are first-team players. They do this by turning their shirts back to front so the photographers can see their surname and squad number. I cannot tell you how much wearing your shirt back to front when you've won something irritates me. So, here it is from me to you: if you have to turn your shirt around for the post-match parade and pictures because you need people to see your name, then you already know that you're not very famous, or not as famous as you want to be, or did not contribute in the way that you should have.

There is a reason why nobody playing regularly in the Premier League does it – it's done by players who want to be famous first and winners second. It's pathetic and worthy of an Instagram account all of its own to call out players who do it.

Just picture it. 'Who's that player with his shirt turned around?' 'Well, it's TSF, obviously.' 'And what trophy is he holding?' 'Hmm ... it looks like the Southern League Central playoff final winners' trophy?' Did I mention that I hate it?

I was happy at that moment. The team were happy. The crowd were happy. It didn't have to have a greater meaning. I didn't have to know what it was all about. Lots of people go through their lives without ever having an uncomplicated moment of happiness like that one was.

These days, people spend a lot of time chasing an awful lot of materialistic shit that doesn't matter. But there are certain things that are worth pursuing in this world and they should always be pursued to nourish your inner happiness.

I may not be the smartest man in the world, or the prettiest, or indeed the wealthiest, and I may move a lot slower nowadays, but it's only because I've realised, many years later, that I don't have to run for anybody anymore.

And when I did run, it was for those moments of happiness. That was my football life and my behavioural experiment.

THE SECRET PSYCHOLOGIST – LAST WORD

Endings are never easy. Footballers are exceptional in many ways, but in this respect they are like the rest of us. At this point, they re-enter our atmosphere.

Imagine having 30 grand a week, 50,000 people chanting your name, and the levels of appreciation, adulation and respect that go with that status ... and then it stops ... and you are 30.

The degree of commitment needed to play football at the highest level is immense. The commitment is even greater if you want to stay there and continue playing at that level. It takes dedication to reach the pinnacle of any sport; no one has ever just wandered round the bottom of a mountain and found themselves at the top.

When footballers retire or lose their career through injury, people often think, 'Well, at least he's got the money.' But in a way this can, believe it or not, make things more difficult for some players. I remember a player saying that he was surrounded by the trappings of a past life. The money and big house were now just part of the legacy.

And I can recall TSF telling me, in one of our many conversations about this book, that there are no pictures of football in his house, no shirts hanging on the wall. He also said that, when his kids play football in the back garden, he doesn't let them wear football shirts because a particular badge on a particular shirt will remind him of an incident at that stadium during a match that he doesn't want to remember. It isn't easy. Money doesn't bury those emotions.

Either way, it is the nervousness and anticipation before the game and the emotional response to the game afterwards that are missed. The neurotransmitters that fire every Saturday (which, by the way, have a certain addictive effect) are where the problem lies.

It is important for players to find a new purpose. A reason for being. The old saying, 'Don't look at it as something ending, look at it as something new starting', is true. More should be done to look after players, who can easily slip into depression or destructive behaviours after retirement. This can either be through career coaching or just ensuring there is more regularity of contact and involvement for club alumni.

Players have to reassess their skills to find their way in the new world. Those skills should, moreover, be assessed and understood in the context of each individual's personality and characteristics. It is important to recognise your skills, because once you are aware of them, you can start thinking how else they can be applied.

I remember asking someone what they did for a living, and she replied, 'I'm just a housewife.' I thought her answer denied her talent. To be a housewife, you have to have people-management skills, negotiation skills, time-management knowledge, budgeting and planning abilities, confidence etc. To be a housewife takes a lot of talent! Likewise, to have played in the Premier League for 10 years as part of a team, you would have skills in negotiation, communication, empathy, strategy ... and the list goes on.

Players who have a good support network, who are surrounded by people who understand the potential psychological impact of severing such an intense career, will do well.

The transition may be helped by the player staying in control of certain aspects of his old life, such as his fitness. To continue to train for another goal, a marathon maybe, keeps the player connected to some familiar aims.

TSF has brought us on a journey (with lots of stop-offs to look at things that interest him) through a footballing life, from beginning to end. For me, as a psychologist and a football fan, the takeaway lesson has to be: how can you make your chances of succeeding (at sport, at a career, whatever) *better*?

I will now perform the old psychologist's trick of answering a question by asking another question.

So, answer this question:

Do you know someone who could be performing better? It might be in the workplace, a family member or someone in your football team.

But here's the thing. I don't mean someone who could perform better by acquiring new skills, going back to college or learning new languages, but just by seeing themselves differently. Maybe by seeing what they do, or who they do it for, differently. I bet you do.

You see, we often think that the route to better performance is through upskilling. We believe we become better by trying to gain greater technical expertise. This is not necessarily always the case. In a way, it's not what we know that is important; it's how we think about what we know.

There is a story that I am reminded of at this point. I've always called this story 'acres of diamonds'. It is a true story. A hundred years or so ago, during the diamond rush in southern Africa, people were tempted to join the big prospectors and to go out and look for diamonds.

A farmer decided to sell his land and buy all the things he needed to go looking for diamonds. He went off and never came back. He never found his fortune and eventually died penniless and alone when he drowned himself in a river. Meanwhile, the people who bought his land cultivated it, and found acres of diamonds – including, at the time, the second-largest diamond in the world.

He had sold the very thing he had gone to look for.

Success is often under our feet, or, more accurately, already within us. We have more than we already need to perform. And yet so often we seem to look outside of ourselves – as if our success exists somewhere else, and if only we could find it ...

We are all too busy spending time thinking about what we haven't got, what we should have done, what could be better. But the truth is, we are already what we need to be, and just need to appreciate and realise our talent a little more. Being better at anything is about understanding the mindsets and attitudes that enable you to perform at your best. Introspection and self-awareness will always allow you to maximise your ability.

And remember – improvement is a game of continual adjustment. Stay learning, questioning and experiencing, and remain open-minded to the power of possibility. I wish you well on your journey.

I leave you with a present. I hope it might be useful.

MY TOP 10 TIPS FOR PLAYING GREAT FOOTBALL (AND ACHIEVING OTHER SUCCESSES)!

1. Be motivated by what you want to achieve, not by what you want to avoid. Trying to move away from failure only brings us closer to it, because we are drawn towards our dominant thoughts. If you take a penalty and think,

'Don't scuff it' or 'Don't hit it wide', you are simply creating pictures of it happening and programming your mind to achieve that negative goal. We are what we think about – so think successful outcomes.

2. Wishing and hoping is not believing. The best players have a genuine belief in their ability. This is not dependent upon results or outcomes; their confidence remains constant because they know that 'to have belief' or 'to have confidence' is a choice. Your thoughts are your own; no one can make you feel something unless you allow them to. Exercise choosing to feel *what* you want to feel, *when* you want to feel it.

3. Blame looks backwards, and responsibility looks forwards. We can blame the surface, the ref, the opposition, our teammates, our boots, our shirts, the weather ... the list is endless. The best players don't spend their time in the circle of circumstance; they spend their time in the circle of influence. Always ask yourself: what can I do in response to situations and circumstances in order to optimise my talent? Don't be a victim of situations. Take responsibility for success.

4. Experience failure and enjoy it! Failure is part payment for success. The price of success is always paid in full and in advance. How can you be a great corner taker unless you take corners? Some of them won't come off. We learn by doing and fucking up. As long as we see everything as an opportunity to learn, there is no such thing as success or failure, just feedback. How has this game made you

better? Muhammad Ali said that 'If a man knows at 50 what he knew at 20, he's wasted 30 years.' If you know what you knew at the beginning of the 90 minutes, you've wasted an opportunity to be better.

5. Detach the action from the person. You can make a mistake, it doesn't make you a mistake; you can experience failure, it doesn't make you a failure. We spend too many days beating ourselves up over what we should have done, what we could have had ... Don't bother. It only conspires to make you feel shit about yourself. The golfer who wins the Masters this year will not be the golfer who makes the fewest mistakes; it will be the golfer who deals best with the mistakes he does make. Follow up a mistake by making great choices.

6. Cultivate a winning demeanour, and stay away from moaners. Be a winner who creates other winners. The way you are in the locker room, the way you put on your boots, the way you listen to the team talk should make all your teammates feel grateful you're on their side. The best players I have seen have a 'presence': Nicolas Anelka, Didier Drogba, Carlos Tevez. Try to act in a way that would allow someone who doesn't know anything about football to walk into the locker room and, just by watching, pick you out as the best player. Be a good teammate; you'll get the support back.

7. Develop a good pre-match routine. Consistency of mind gets you consistency of play. When you are playing great, it is not a purple patch or 'good form'; it is how you can

play all the time. The rest of the time you have 'interference'. Interference is thoughts that are compromising your performance. Something is getting in the way of your natural talent. What is the commonality in your thinking when you have a good game? Create a framework for your pre-game thinking – and, no, this is not about superstitions! They don't count.

8. Practise, practise, practise – and, when it is perfect, practise some more. It is no coincidence that the best sportspeople in the world practise more than anyone else. Confidence comes from the replication of tasks to a consistently high standard. Get it right so many times that you don't need convincing you can do it. And don't just practise technique, practise the mindset you need for different occasions. What will you be thinking when you're 2–0 down with five minutes to play? You should know ...

9. Never weaken a strength to strengthen a weakness. Arsène Wenger said that great players have great self-awareness – he was right. Know what you are good at. Whole careers have been made in a variety of sports by players who were technically compromised. They understood their strengths, no matter how limited, and used them to their full potential. Sometimes, when we focus upon our weaknesses, it simply makes us feel bad. Understand your strong points and make them stronger. Remember, it is easier to take something from good to great than get something from bad to good.

10. Create a brand. Think very clearly and simply what you want to be known for – what is your brand of football? Once you label yourself as something, it is easier to become it. Our minds are like soil: whatever thought you plant will take root and grow. Unfortunately, most of us think in the negative. See yourself as 'the hardest-working striker on the pitch' – there is a simplicity to your brand that will make it true. It might be that a midfielder thinks, 'I stop my opposing number from playing.' Whatever it is, make sure it is something you can 'roll up' and take anywhere. No matter what the match situation or the weather conditions, home or away – this is what you stand for. Make sure the opposition know it at the end of the game.

Good luck!

INDEX